It was only a matter of time before a clever publisher realized that there is an audience for whom *Exile on Main Street* or *Electric Ladyland* are as significant and worthy of study as *The Catcher in the Rye* or *Middlemarch* . . . The series . . . is freewheeling and eclectic, ranging from minute rock-geek analysis to idiosyncratic personal celebration — *The New York Times Book Review*

Ideal for the rock geek who thinks liner notes just aren't enough — *Rolling Stone*

One of the coolest publishing imprints on the planet — *Bookslut*

These are for the insane collectors out there who appreciate fantastic design, well-executed thinking, and things that make your house look cool. Each volume in this series takes a seminal album and breaks it down in startling minutiae. We love these. We are huge nerds — *Vice*

A brilliant series . . . each one a work of real love — *NME* (UK)

Passionate, obsessive, and smart — *Nylon*

Religious tracts for the rock 'n' roll faithful — *Boldtype*

[A] consistently excellent series — *Uncut* (UK)

We . . . aren't naive enough to think that we're your only source for reading about music (but if we had our way . . . watch out). For those of you who really like to know everything there is to know about an album, you'd do well to check out Bloomsbury's "33 1/3" series of books — *Pitchfork*

**For reviews of individual titles in the series, please visit our blog at 333sound.com and our website at www.bloomsbury.com/musicandsoundstudies**

**Follow us on Twitter: @333books**

**Like us on Facebook: www.facebook.com/33.3books**

For a complete list of books in this series, see the back of this book.

# Once Upon a Time

BLOOMSBURY ACADEMIC
Bloomsbury Publishing Inc
1385 Broadway, New York, NY 10018, USA
50 Bedford Square, London, WC1B 3DP, UK
29 Earlsfort Terrace, Dublin 2, Ireland

BLOOMSBURY, BLOOMSBURY ACADEMIC and the Diana logo are
trademarks of Bloomsbury Publishing Plc

First published in the United States of America 2021

Copyright © Alex Jeffery, 2021

All rights reserved. No part of this publication may be reproduced or
transmitted in any form or by any means, electronic or mechanical, including
photocopying, recording, or any information storage or retrieval system,
without prior permission in writing from the publishers.

Bloomsbury Publishing Inc does not have any control over, or responsibility
for, any third-party websites referred to or in this book. All internet
addresses given in this book were correct at the time of going to press.
The author and publisher regret any inconvenience caused if addresses
have changed or sites have ceased to exist but can accept no
responsibility for any such changes.

Library of Congress Cataloging-in-Publication Data

ISBN: PB:      978-1-5013-5546-2
       ePDF:   978-1-5013-5548-6
       eBook:  978-1-5013-5547-9

Series: 33 1/3

Typeset by RefineCatch Limited, Bungay, Suffolk
Printed and bound in the United States of America

To find out more about our authors and books visit
www.bloomsbury.com and sign up for our newsletters.

# Once Upon a Time

**33⅓**

## Alex Jeffery

BLOOMSBURY ACADEMIC
NEW YORK · LONDON · OXFORD · NEW DELHI · SYDNEY

*For J*

*The sweetest fantasist I ever knew*

*Live happily ever after*

# Contents

# Introduction
## Once Upon A Time

*Once Upon A Time, the great music of the cosmos breathed a new pattern into existence. As the music evolved, the dreamweavers, craftspeople gifted with the knowledge of music, learned how to thread it into a tapestry of sound. Unbroken, it flowed like a river. Through the night, people loved to dance to the music, forgetting all their troubles until they washed up exhausted but happy on the shores of morning. In the city of New York, great palaces were built, so that many could join together in the dance. Here, you could live out your fantasies, and love whomsoever you chose, bathed in the scintillation" of a million spinning lights. Especially revered among the singers of this music were the women—ravishing" queens who sang of love, hearts broken and the joy of dancing. Disco was loved by many, but also hated in equal measure. Threatened by its success, a council of white men formed to see what could be done. It was said that the real cause of their hatred were disco's ardent disciples—blacks, latinos, gays and women. And so, a plan was hatched to destroy it. One afternoon, the council held a great gathering, inviting people from far across the land. "Bring your disco records" they said "and we will burn them."*

*Their plan worked, and news soon spread of disco's demise. All of a sudden, sad and unwanted, it disappeared from the land. But it was not forgotten. Deep underground, the flame was kept alive by a cult of beautiful faeries. Ecstatically, they danced around it, drawing pleasure from its warmth. There, disco waited patiently until the day when it could return to the light, and everyone would once again dance to its tune. Fortunately, beautiful things have a habit of not staying concealed for too long, though" like spring flowers pushing up after the long winter, disco music tentatively came back to the surface. There it was greeted like a long-lost friend. Those who couldn't love it at least tolerated it, and disco took its place in the pantheon of music eternal. There it lived and prospered, happily ever after.*

... and so the story goes. When *I* discovered disco as a teenager in the late 1980s, and forged my own bond with it, the nails had still not quite been prised from its coffin. Declared dead at the start of the decade when white male rock-ness reasserted its primacy, towards the end disco albums clogged up the bargain bins of second-hand record stores. Jostling for inattention alongside easy-listening landfill and other pop failures of yesterday, you could pick them up in the UK for a pound or two. In any case, disco was never really shunned in the UK, at least not compared to the American mainstream. You could trace our more conciliatory relationship in the singles charts, through which disco remakes, remixes, samples and homages occasionally migrated throughout the 1980s and into the 1990s.[1]

---

[1] First there was Patrick Cowley's remix of "I Feel Love" at the end of 1982, then an unexpected Sister Sledge revival in 1984; torch-bearer Jimmy

One record that had never gone out of fashion was Donna Summer's "I Feel Love." I was personally fascinated by it—and, well, frankly who *wasn't*.

It was enough reason to take home a copy of *I Remember Yesterday* out of sheer curiosity and soon, I found myself out of step with my teenage peers, who were immersed deep in a Fleetwood Mac revival. I snapped up all the disco-era albums Summer had made with her producers Giorgio Moroder and Pete Bellotte at Musicland Studios, names that to me then became objects of curiosity in their own right. I liked the albums well enough, although sometimes I suspected that the concepts were rather flimsy. *Once Upon A Time* was different, though—a whole other kettle of glitter that pressed on my budding queer sensibilities and gave me something to get my teeth into. There weren't exactly many double concept albums around during the 1980s, and nothing much appealed to me about progressive rock, which had somehow managed to make itself even less fashionable than disco. The cod-surrealism of the prog cover art looked like drippy fantasy to me, but Donna Summer's simply staged album cover drew me like a moth to a blue flame. Its immediate queer appeal is summed up neatly by another admirer, Jimmy Somerville, whose first band, Bronski Beat, invaded charts worldwide with the gay-storied "Smalltown Boy" in 1984.

Somerville charted high with disco covers in 1985, 1986, and 1987 while in 1988, disco-sampling arrived via the UK house number one "Theme From S'Express." Eventually, this tipped into full-tilt global revival peaking around 1994, coinciding with the new hit compilation *Endless Summer: Donna Summer's Greatest Hits.*

Somerville recollects that: "when I bought *Once Upon a Time* and I opened the sleeve and I saw Donna Summer in that big white dress sprinkling stardust across Manhattan, I was like 'Oh! My! God!'" What's more, beyond its luminous sleeve, the album looked like it might have a proper story—the kind of thing I personally loved.

Recently I read a review by *The Guardian's* Michael Hann (of Linda Ortega's 2018 album *Liberty* as it happens) which summed up a universal issue with concept albums: "Ortega sings a story that—as with most song cycles and concept albums—doesn't really make a lot of sense unless someone explains it to you." There's a lot of truth in this statement, but it really doesn't apply to *Once Upon a Time*, the concept album with a story you *can* follow on first listen. The concept, taken at face value, is straightforward—a retelling of the Cinderella fable, updated to a contemporary disco setting in New York. That's largely it, and the story archetype over which it's built is familiar to all. Unlike most narrative concept albums, you're not immediately challenged with something to puzzle over and decode through the act of listening. There's no lofty pretention, none of the very male conceptual rigor that brought *The Lamb Lies Down on Broadway* or *Close to the Edge* into being. Yet what at first comes across as a simple fairy tale turns out to be deceptively complex, a text that invites you to keep returning. The music is masterfully complex in itself. Scintillating with light one minute, inhabiting some very dank, lonely corners the next, the *NME's* Angus McKinnon described the seamless mix and merge of different moods and modes as "chameleon but never caricature." At its center is a fascinatingly dysfunctional character, one of the most psychologically complex of all Cinderella's. What drew me ever further into the album was how all this managed to chime with the isolation and teenage angst going on in my own life—more so than any album by The Smiths. Over time, through repeated listening, new mysteries kept unfolding. It felt that there was always more story under the surface, as if the songs were just the audible tip of the iceberg. The more time I spent with the record, the more nuances I discovered, the more I felt, thought, *imagined*.

It's ironic to think now about where disco ended up, as an immovable pillar among the firmament of the great pop genres. It unites generations at weddings, and for pop stars trying to diversify their sound by ransacking the past, it's an invaluable resource, a touchstone even. As such, disco has arguably endured better than all its contemporaries. In her (favorable) *Sounds* review of *Once Upon A Time*, Jane Suck described most disco as "disposable: a musical Durex." Yet, as a classic singles medium, the best disco tracks haven't just lasted; occupying a considerable cultural footprint, they have triumphed, having the last laugh over those who thought they were just mass-produced ephemera. But what about disco *albums*? That's quite another matter. In the afterlife of disco, its albums are often thought of as flimsy product more than art, cobbled together from a few choice dancefloor cuts and padded out with filler. The more outlandish disco albums have developed reputations as cult curios, to be hawked semi-ironically around the blogosphere by the crate-digging cognoscenti of camp. That they dared to aspire to the grandiosity of the concept album can often seem ridiculous in retrospect, but for some this makes their appreciation all the more juicy: voyages into outer space, exoticized fantasies of African queens and Arabian nights, lofty adaptations of Shakespeare—the hallmarks are there of progressive rock's indulgence, without much of the implied musical complexity. Imagine, then, a writer doing something as frivolous as taking a disco album seriously enough to write about one in depth. Right there for you is an exercise in hipsterdom if ever there was one. Making a disco album a subject for a book seems to fly in the face of everything the music was about— the feet, the body, the company of other, preferably very sweaty, people. It certainly wasn't designed for the same living room contemplation of *Dark Side of the Moon*—cross legged, reverent, cerebral. Nevertheless, that's exactly what this book is going to do; and along the way it will point out a few areas where disco and prog aren't perhaps as oppositional as you might imagine. It asks you to take a more measured consideration of the disco album, by re-examining the one work that might well be its greatest achievement—Donna Summer's double-disc fairy tale *Once Upon A Time*.

It's easy to forget exactly where disco was positioned in the album market, so let's start with a few facts, and perhaps alter a few misconceptions. As the American 1970s drew to a close, the genre, still less than a decade old, had become a commercial juggernaut, bringing in huge revenues for the record industry from sales of both singles (including the recently developed twelve-inch format) *and* albums. By the middle of 1979, disco had risen to rival rock as the predominant genre in the *Billboard* albums chart, although its victory turned out to be short-lived. Soon afterwards, having flown too close to the sun, and perhaps too fast, it fell swiftly and infamously from grace. The reasons were manifold. The Disco Sucks movement, which allowed latent aggressions against the genre to come into the open, certainly didn't help.[2] It was also partly due to sheer overexposure and the bandwagon-jumping of unsuitable artists trying to cash in (*The Ethel Merman Disco Album* being the most notorious example). Yet before the fall was complete, one of its artists managed a remarkable feat—she became the only act to achieve *three Billboard* number one double albums inside a decade. Looking back, that it was a disco singer (black and female) who achieved this and not one of the titans of progressive rock (invariably white and male) is quite astonishing. As if Donna Summer's hat trick of releases (*Live and More* in 1978, *Bad Girls* and *On the Radio: Greatest Hits Volumes I & II* in 1979) wasn't impressive enough by itself, she achieved them one after the other within a fourteen-month period—proof of the hurricane force of her success at the time.

Here are some further eye-opening sales facts: *Saturday Night Fever* is not only the biggest selling disco album of all time, but thought to be the biggest selling soundtrack ever, with 50 million-plus units worldwide. The list of platinum hits in disco goes on and on including albums by Diana Ross, Sister Sledge, Rose Royce, Gloria Gaynor, multiple releases from Chic, Kool and the Gang, and The Village People, not to

---

[2] Fun fact: After Steve Dahl's infamous "Disco Demolition Night" at Comisky Park in Chicago on July 12, 1979, it was Donna Summer's "Last Dance" that was chosen to signal disco's destruction. It was played for twenty-four hours straight on Chicago's WLUP station before they declared disco dead.

mention the Gibb industrial complex of the Bee Gees and their little brother Andy. By the time the 20 million-selling *Off the Wall* arrived, Michael Jackson had effectively become a disco artist, and disco effectively underpins most of the biggest selling album of all time—*Thriller*. So, yes, disco certainly *was* an "album genre," even if its brief time in the sun led to premature burnout. Album sales do not necessarily imply quality, though, and at different stages in the lifespan of the genre, descent into crass formula threatened to drag disco down. At the start of 1976, Vince Aletti's regular column in *Record World* magazine, which for several years provided an insider's commentary on disco releases, spewed out an extraordinary rant on the subject. Aletti lamented how disco music's "willingness to take recording studio soul to its limits; its unpredictability; its weirdness" had been eased out in favor of a plague of disco remakes. Many of these records ghoulishly revived the standards of yesteryear, helping push the budding genre towards "the lowest, most laughable form of pop music; the muzak of the seventies." But by August the same year, Aletti had backtracked spectacularly, citing a new wave of productions (including the far more sophisticated throwback Dr. Buzzard's Original Savannah Band) as possible saviors, and the expanding catalog of disco's brightest hope, Donna Summer also seemed to point the way forward. The "unexpected, complex, irresistibly involving music" that had attracted disco's ardent fans in the first place was now back in the game. By the end of 1976, disco had survived stagnating formulas and "its own baddish popularity" to have one of its most creative years. Then, in 1977, its longevity seemed finally sealed by an influx of innovative albums coming out of disco's new centers of production, among them Paris, London, and the new European cultural hotspot of Munich.

It was towards the end of this year that one of them prepared to make its grand entrance to the ball as disco's first magnum opus. *Once Upon A Time* didn't arrive fully formed out of nowhere but was the latest in a series of conceptual album experiments created by the Munich-based team of Donna Summer, Giorgio Moroder, and Pete Bellotte. In the double album, for the first time in disco music, a single, unified concept stretched out across four sides of vinyl. Its scale and creative ambition was a reflection of the confidence of its producers and artist that there was a place for such product in the market. The rock critics, particularly those at *Rolling Stone,* could be exceptionally sniffy about disco, but by the release of *Once Upon A Time* on October 31, it seemed even they were softening towards the idea. Donna Summer already had form with her previous album *I Remember Yesterday*, which helped pave the road away from the cliché and stagnation that sometimes made disco easy for rockists to dismiss. Wittily repurposing the past, it also beamed at warp-speed into the future with the hit "I Feel Love," a recording which has been endlessly cited as changing electronic music forever. It began to look like the versatile star and the inventive and experienced production team behind her might just have the goods to usher in a new era. With the follow-up, *LA Times'* Robert Hilburn positioned her as ready to leave the "artistically vapid herd" of other disco acts far behind. If for some, a double concept album coming out of disco provoked a certain amount of skepticism, this all melted away for Hilburn when he heard the album's "sheer record-making craft." *The New York Times'* John Rockwell saw fit to proclaim it as disco's "artistic coming of age" and, in an article for the Boston Globe, one of disco's most celebrated commentators, Richard Dyer, understood the album as using "disco as a point of departure." Suddenly, it seemed as if the genre held serious possibilities for the future. Where would it depart to? And how high could it aim?

Everything seemed to be gesturing towards commercial success, but *Once Upon A Time* wasn't quite the big breakthrough many predicted. In the week that it entered the *Billboard* album chart at number 48, a rival disco-double came in one place higher at 47—the soundtrack to *Saturday Night Fever*. The following January, as the Donna Summer album reached its peak of number 26, *Saturday Night Fever* spent the first of twenty-four weeks at the top. It seemed that mass audiences *were* interested in disco as a storytelling medium, just not the one that had piqued the attention of the critics. Eclipsed by an unexpected cultural titan, *Once Upon A Time* still managed to kick around in the Top 200 for the entire year, becoming 1978's thirty-second biggest album overall. It was Summer's highest position to-date on the year-end charts but the longed-for mainstream embrace and recognition of her talent still hadn't arrived. As the decades pass, the reputation of the album is still somewhat undernourished. Evidenced by Pete Bellotte's royalty statements, it's the "least performing" of the albums he and Moroder produced for their main star. It houses none of her most loved hits ("Love to Love You Baby," "Bad Girls," "Hot Stuff," "I Feel Love," "Last Dance," "Macarthur Park") and the long running time perhaps presents too formidable a barrier to the casual buyer. Go rooting around inside the Donna Summer fan community, however, and things start to look a little different. When discussed in forums and niche online polls, which it often is, the album quickly emerges as a firm favorite, rivaled only by her biggest seller, *Bad Girls*.

If you ask people why they love the album so much, naturally they will all give different answers, have different songs that mean something to them. That's no surprise—*Once Upon A Time* is rich in subtexts, and it connects to many areas of *life*. As you read this book, many of these subtexts will be explored, from its inner-city setting in the late 1970s to its unlikely connections to progressive rock. It also puts a queer eye on the story, one that is inspired by my own experiences travelling through life. But most obviously, there's no way round the fact that you're listening to a Cinderella story, and there are a *lot* of other Cinderella tales out there for it to connect to, musical or otherwise. Although fairy stories have simple enough words and structures, there's a reason why the most well-worn ones remain popular—they tap into our biggest fears and desires. *Once Upon A Time* puts its own spin on them and takes us down some quite peculiar psychological avenues. It also happens to be a fairy story sung by a black woman, and there are issues that need investigating around that too.

Along the way, I've created a few fairy stories of my own, mostly because it just felt like the right thing to do. Fairy stories aren't really so far away from myths—narratives that the more they get repeated, crystallize the pliability of whatever the truth once was. Disco has its own myths as well—perhaps this book will contribute to them.

# 1
# Sweet Romance:
# A Tale of Two Discos

"My greatest gift as a singer-songwriter has always been
telling stories".
— *Donna Summer – Ordinary Girl.*

Here's a quick thought experiment. Let's imagine picking up
a copy of *Once Upon A Time* blind out of a record bin with no
previous knowledge of the artist. Let's then imagine trying to
work out where it came from. What are our clues? Probably,
your eyes would be drawn first to the radiant singer on the
front cover. You *might* assume her, whether it's fair or not, to
be an American. After all, it's 1977, she's black and making an
expensively packaged double album. Next, scan the title
captions "Once Upon A Time" and "Happily Ever After" on
the front and back. The fairy tale theme is there, obviously,
but the signature baby blue and ivory color scheme are
borrowed from Disney's animated *Cinderella* film, which
hints at an Americanized rather than European approach to
the subject matter. Opening the gatefold sleeve, you're struck
by a startling image—a giant version of the star towers over a

silhouette of the Manhattan skyline at sunset. Like an "attack-of-the-50-foot-Disney-heroine," she sprinkles a shower of stars over the skyscape. There's also a text to accompany the image; the earnest talk of fighting odds and striving to achieve your dreams is a hymn, perhaps, to the American Dream. It's only by scanning the back of the lyric sheet that you would discover where the album was actually recorded—Munich in southern Germany. If you then still assumed it to be of German origin, you'd have missed a lot of the detail. Studying the credits further reveals the album was produced by an Italian (Giorgio Moroder) and co-written by a man with a French-sounding name (Pete Bellotte), who is, in fact, from England.

The other musicians on the record, not that you'd necessarily know it, are a mix of Europeans (including English, German, Swedish and French), alongside some Americans, most notably the female back-up singers. OK, let's now return to the singer—Donna Summer. Although African-American, she'd been building a career in Germany since the late 1960s, first on the stage and then as a recording artist. By now, she's moved back to the States as her pop career takes off, but she's still committed to recording in Germany where her producers are. As the needle hits the opening grooves of the record, the style is unambiguously disco, if a rather melodramatic version of it. But what kind of disco artist makes a double album based on a fairy tale and organizes it into four "acts," one for each side?

If there's a lesson to be learned from this confusion, it's that disco was a *transnational* phenomenon. The back and forward cultural exchange in disco happened mostly across the

Atlantic. *Once Upon A Time* was emblematic of the process, as was Donna Summer, the "extraordinary pneumatic icon created and patented in a German laboratory" and "trans-American goddess of the computer age" as Barney Hoskyns fruitily put it in 1982. As the disco industry expanded during the 1970s, its centers of production on America's seaboards (New York, Boston, Philadelphia) became increasingly entangled with newer ones in key European cities. The global disco network was complex, and it encompassed many different nodes. Recording studios, record companies and musicians all had a part to play, as did audiences and the places where the music was mostly played—the discothèques themselves. The new records coming out of the Old World couldn't really be said to be "pure" in their European origin, but the media was quick to hive the newcomer off into a new subgenre, with characteristics distinct from its American cousin. As imports began to flood into America from late 1975, a new term was coined. "Eurodisco," as it became known, was both disdained by critics for its precision naffness and welcomed by DJs for its fresh sounds and structural innovations. American disco captured a visceral "now"—the sweat of the dancefloor, the unfiltered tears and joy of the love/sexual relationship. In contrast, a lot of its European counterpart seemed intent on escaping the present moment into a kind of disco fantasia. Some Eurodisco set off on a jet-set musical odyssey around the globe—each track on the first two albums of French band Voyage landed in a specific locale (Indonesia, Scotland, the Deep South) to exploit the local flavor like a disco Dr. Livingstone. Others harked back to a classical era of storytelling, referencing ancient history or attempting to adapt Shakespeare. Then there were those musicians transported away by the thrill of technology and science fiction pulp. In parallel with the wilder Afro-futurist funk coming from America, they blasted upwards and outwards into the future. Sci-fi disco's greatest hit, Cerrone's "Supernature," managed to be inspired by both the past and the future, updating H.G. Wells' 1896 novel *The Island of Dr. Moreau* for the new hi-tech disco world.

The greatest European disco producer of all, Giorgio Moroder, was the transnationality of disco personified. Rather than sit tight in his Munich studio-fortress, receiving visiting singers and musicians like a king in his court, he went where he was needed to make records happen, taking advantage of the fast-developing transnational disco networks. Constantly on the move between Munich, Paris, London, New York, and Los Angeles, his colleagues eventually coined the phrase "En Route Moroder" (on the Moroder road) to describe his work pattern. Munich may have been where his studio was, but his permanent home was in Switzerland "not for tax reasons, but because I like it there." During the 1990s, at a low career ebb, he granted an interview to *Eurotrash*, the British 1990s TV show that gently poked fun at all things continental. The origins of disco, he maintained, weren't American but essentially European, the continent where "we did disco kind of music way before"; the discothèque, in its simplest definition a nightclub where disc jockeys played records in sequence for dancing, had, after all, evolved in France. There was some truth in the claim but ignoring disco's roots within the marginalized African and Latin American communities of New York was insensitive.

Most likely, his diminished cultural role at the time of the interview had made him defensive, but his position was not always so. In 1978, at the peak of his success he gave a far more nuanced account to the *NME*. "This matter of a European feeling is really quite complicated," he maintained, arguing that any perception of "Europeanness" in his work came down to a sound training in continental pop music in the pre-disco years. Any "European leaning" in the Moroder disco sound was simply projection—the music was only European in the sense that it was created there. Somewhere between the two rhetorical positions, perhaps, dwells what Eurodisco really is. Things are complicated further by European disco producers who relocated to the States, as did the writer/producer double act of two Moroccan-born Frenchmen, Jacques Morali and Henri Belolo. Operating out of New York, they also started making disco records in Philadelphia and soon had their breakthrough act— American-born singing non-sisters, The Ritchie Family, whose debut hit with "Brazil," was Morali's idea of doing a Busby Berkeley-inspired disco version of Ary Barroso's "Aquarela do Brasil." Fed by Morali's often fertile imagination, they went on to pantomime their way through a series of exotic tableaux of *African Queens* and *Arabian Nights*. These were fantasies too lurid for any American producer to have thought of at the time, but the Frenchmen's greatest fantasy of all was an outsider's reimagining of America itself. Inspired by visits to gay bars around Greenwich Village, the four songs on the debut album from Village People were all odes to American gay hotspots of the 1970s. The hyper-masculine archetypes of Village People were sold back to middle

America, who were largely unaware of their original context in gay clone culture. Morali even recontextualized the historical charge of the pioneers in the clarion call of "Go West" to sexually liberated San Francisco.[1] With European producers moving in to shape Americans' understanding of themselves, had European disco simply *become* American disco? And how might you even tell the difference?

Back in Europe, there were centers of production right across the continent. Germany had disco-producing studios in Frankfurt, Offenbach, and Cologne, as well as the now legendary Hansa Tonstudio in Berlin. Paris housed Studios Ferber, where the production team of Jean Kluger and Daniel Vangard turned out hits for the Gibson Brothers and Ottowan. Even Belgium had its own disco specialization—an Afro/Latin sound that produced very un-European sounding records like Chakachas' "Jungle Fever" and Bad Blood's "Aie A Mwana." But the disco capital of Europe, and one of its main cultural hubs in the 1970s, was indisputably Munich, with numerous studios alongside its main disco-hub Musicland, including Arco, Studio 70, Country Lane and Union, where Frank Farian recorded his key act Boney M. As early as 1975, the first wave of disco imports from Europe hit America. France provided Crystal Grass' "Crystal World" and the cod-Spanish sound of Bimbo Jet's "El Bimbo," while Germany served up hits from Silver Convention like "Save Me" and "Fly Robin Fly." The latter became the first number

---

[1] Curiously, Morali's 1978 concept album about Josephine Baker (*Josephine Superstar,* sung by later Cosby show star Phylicia Allen) charts the reverse march eastwards, as Baker passes through "St. Louis" and "Broadway," en route to success and infamy in Paris.

one on the Hot 100 from a European disco production house, a fact pointed out by Vince Aletti's *Record World* column, now an invaluable month-by-month document of when and how imports arrived. Aletti first used the term "Eurodisco" in his column at the end of 1977, which he proclaimed as "import music's hottest year." In an outbreak of bidding wars, almost every major European record had been "snatched up for American release almost as soon as it broke." Although far from all European acts managed to replicate their home success in America, the stream of imports was often likened to an invasion, and a barbarian one at that. American critics sharpened their claws. *Village Voice* scribe Robert Christgau, owner of one of the more vicious sets of talons, was fairly well disposed to disco in general, but loved to take side-swipes at Eurodisco. He found the bad lyrics in *Take The Heat Off Me,* the debut album from Boney M. unintentionally funny, and its "tinkly-shit" choices of American covers (like Neil Young's "Heart of Gold") sounded to his ears "calculated, as if produced by some fantastic cuckoo clock." Silver Convention's lyrics, meanwhile, were "so simple-minded they couldn't have been devised by anyone who knows English as a native language."

Enjoying disco has long been an area of contested taste, but a foul whiff of suspicion has lingered around Eurodisco in particular, which has only condensed over the years. Peter Shapiro's history of disco *Turn the Beat Around* characterizes the style as coming out of Europe "like a marauding Ostrogoth in clodhoppers and a three-piece polyester suit." Such crude stereotyping goes too far, especially given the complexities of Eurodisco's transnationality, but closer up there are at least some broad distinguishing characteristics to be identified. As early as 1975, Aletti could identify a particularly "European flavor" to the records flying in from Germany. Silver Convention's records, for example, were prized for their combination of crisp sweeps of scything strings with electronics, all housed within an overall crystal-clear production. As this was Germany, there was still a tendency for all kinds of unfortunate national stereotypes to emerge from the woodwork. The new precision-tooled sound was sometimes called "Teutonic disco" and, in later appraisals, this was even more grossly caricatured as "goose-stepping stomp beats and beer-hall sing-alongs" (Shapiro again). It's interesting to note that Moroder, who now often gets discussed in serious books on German popular music alongside Kraftwerk, Neu and Tangerine Dream, railed against the idea of any supposed "German sound" in disco. In fact, the mere idea of it provoked him to bang his fists on the desk in an interview, before listing the musicians involved (including himself, Bellotte, Boney M., Summer and her label-mate Roberta Kelly) who weren't actually German themselves. Ironically, the steady, driving four-to-the-floor bass thump so prized in his records was produced by Musicland's drummer in residence Keith Forsey—no goose-stepping German, but an Englishman.[2] Moroder also refused to accept that, as a location, Munich possessed any magic ingredients for success. This, he felt, would probably have come sooner in London, thanks to its

---

[2] Forsey later forged a career as rock/pop producer in his own right, including the first four Billy Idol albums and Simple Minds' soundtrack smash "Don't You Forget About Me."

better facilities and proximity to the "pulse of the industry." So much for Teutonic disco.

When Moroder and Bellotte scored their first big disco hit in 1975 with Summer's "Love to Love You Baby," two of Eurodisco's other characteristics emerged with it. Firstly, there was the frank expression of sex, which came about from Moroder's desire to create a disco equivalent to the scandalous softcore pop of Serge Gainsbourg and Jane Birkin's "Je T'Aime (Moi Non Plus)" from 1969. The preoccupation with ... ahem ... length was the result of a request from Summer's label boss Neil Bogart, who, legend has it, was looking for a new soundtrack for his bedroom. The long version of the song teased the new genre out into an extended opus that, at seventeen minutes, could stand proudly alongside the most self-indulgent rock music. It filled the first half of her second album of the same name, launching her as an album artist at the same time as the single climbed to number two. After "Love to Love You Baby" unexpectedly conquered worldwide, extending your opus quickly became the thing. Its chart success was a milestone in disco, giving the green light to all manner of conceptual disco "suites." The Frenchman Marc Cerrone grabbed the baton with vigor, serving up another elongated (if speeded up) slab of sex disco in "Love in C Minor." Positioning himself as the DJ-porno king at the center of a one-on-three pile up, Cerrone's sixteen-minute record dovetailed neatly with the erotic films pouring out of the continent during the 1970s. They may have been attention-seeking and sometimes bordering on crass, but the lascivious content in these records belied the sophistication in their arrangement and production. Meanwhile, occupying a side of an LP became *de rigueur* and, at the end of 1977, Aletti praised the stream of "sustained, dramatically structured, intriguingly avant-garde compositions that filled the entire side of the record." They all came from Europe. He singled out three producers as the architects of the disco renaissance: Cerrone and Alec R. Costandinos (both based in France) and the Moroder/Bellotte complex in Munich.

Inevitably, in the era of progressive rock, Eurodisco soon made the move from conceptual one-siders to full-blown concept albums. The "serious" disco album now seems like an oxymoron for a genre now permanently associated with frivolity, but some producers of disco saw it as a medium for exploring some very heady artistic ambitions. Aletti also began each monthly column by gushing over the latest album releases rather than singles. At a time when the market for disco was still far more geared to singles than albums, what did this imply? Could disco albums also serve as pleasurable at-home listening? He remarked that the whole of Silver Convention's *Save Me* was "perfect for at-home atmosphere," but, as an arch-enthusiast, he wasn't really the typical listener. Moroder had a different take and felt that the first album he produced that could "be properly enjoyed at home" didn't happen until 1979: rock band Sparks' attempt at disco with *Number One in Heaven*. As the *NME* pointed out in their interview with him, "Can anyone reasonably expect to review disco sitting down?"

As for the rock critics, they were generally hostile to disco's insistence on the body, which lacked, as writer Tim Lawrence later noted, the two key symbols of rockist authority— "the lead vocalist and the lead guitarist." Early disco albums hedged their bets in the market with a hotchpotch selection of different styles and tempos, hoping that some cuts would be picked up for the dancefloor, others for the radio. To win over the rock critics, the disco album had to evolve. Generally speaking, writers at the magazine "didn't have a clue about disco" as Greil Marcus admitted in *Rolling Stone Magazine: The Uncensored History*. "It was just something everybody hoped would go away." When it arrived, *Once Upon A Time* wasn't so easily dismissed, though, and it garnered a lengthy review by Stephen Holden in *Rolling Stone*, who called it "the *ne plus ultra* of disco albums." In a month when Bowie's *Heroes* was also reviewed, *Once Upon A Time* took precedence—a definitive win for disco over rock. Other critics couldn't help making comparisons with progressive rock. Dave Marsh, another *Rolling Stone* writer, trumpeted it as a "masterpiece" in his review, if somewhat reluctantly. The "fairy tale disco" was "just as imposing in its own silly way" as The Who's *Tommy*, he felt, and in many ways was "more 'artistic' than much of what the European avant-garde has to offer." This strangely upended the high/low art divide in favor of disco. The Who comparison also resonated with Christgau over at the *Village Voice*, who quipped "roll over Pete Townshend and tell Jerry Leiber the news" in his review, drawing attention to the "actual story" printed on the sleeves, just as The Who had done with *Quadrophenia*.

To some extent this was justified as disco and progressive rock actually had a wide plain of musical crossover. The perennial, yet still not quite classifiable favorite, *Jeff Wayne's Musical Version of War of the Worlds* managed an imaginative hybrid of the two, as did the mostly European subgenre of space disco. A less remarked-upon phenomenon is how, in parallel with prog rock, disco increasingly co-opted the language of classical music. After "Love to Love You Baby," suites, preludes, themes, and reprises all began steadily to appear on disco albums. There is a basic logic behind at least some of this. The term "suite," which dates back to the late renaissance, originated in formulating a set series of dance pieces, which varied in tempo and meter. "Prelude" also became part of the language of proto-disco parties at The Loft, where DJ David Mancuso would play softer and more delicate music at the beginning of the night, including Indian ragas, Japanese Koto music and *The Nutcracker*. By incorporating classical structures like the sonata form in Yes' *Close to the Edge*, progressive rock wore its complexity as a badge of honor, daring critics and audiences not to take it seriously. Disco, however, never tried to slavishly graft on the grand organizational structures of centuries past. Instead, it cheekily borrowed the *idea* of them. Camouflage's "A Disco Symphony," an American production, wasn't quite what it said on the tin. The notion of "symphony" here meant a big pot-pourri that threw in all kinds of quotations from Ravel's *Bolero* to *Rhapsody in Blue*, The Supremes' "I Hear a Symphony" and a disco-fied section of "MacArthur Park" (predating Donna Summer's version by a year). It's not that disco's more talented producers didn't understand structure, but they had their own methods of assembling it, more akin to collage. Longer tracks built in different moods, rhythms, key, and tempo changes to prevent the listener and dancer from getting bored—the "turns" that DJs prized for their creative variation. However, the demands of the dancefloor necessitated the continuity of same-tempo sequences, like the celebrated Side A of Gloria Gaynor's 1975 debut *Never Can Say Goodbye*, created by pioneering disco mixer Tom Moulton. Treading the fine line between similarity and difference was key in making long disco tracks work (the "mini musical masterpiece" that Tom Moulton aimed for in his suites), as well as crafting a compelling side to an LP.

In an often-clumsy rapprochement with classical music, as the disco boom really took off in 1976, both sides of the Atlantic applied themselves to disco remakes of its best-known tunes. It's an odd historical quirk, which ended ignominiously in the cookie-cutter schlock of the *Hooked on Classics* series. Along the way, though, it turned out some genuinely inventive music like The Philharmonics "1812 Overture," which slyly inverts one of the most bombastic pieces ever composed into a swaggering, slow strut. Beethoven perhaps would have preferred his deafness to Walter Murphy's chart topping "A Fifth of Beethoven," but the funky clavinet comping that answers the "ta-ta-ta-taaaaaa" fate motif is a brilliantly pithy musical joke, as well as a stone cold throw down.[3] The reach-back into the past wasn't restricted to the canon of Western art music, and literature got its dues as well. The aspirant high priest of disco storytelling was Alec R. Costandinos, a producer whose heritage had already crossed many borders. Born in Egypt to Armenian/Greek parents, an Irish Catholic school education in Cairo provided his early

---

[3] Other productions were more lamentable, with clod-hopping orchestra leaders like Arthur Fiedler (and the Boston Pops) slumming it for easy cash on *Saturday Night Fiedler*. Eine Kleine Disco Band's 1978 album *Disco Saturday Nacht (Feverish Sounds of 1830)* is worth a look for one of the funniest album covers of all time—a recreation of the *Saturday Night Fever* cover with a bewigged young Mozart pulling the signature Travolta move. The music, surprisingly, is actually quite passable.

introduction to Shakespeare. After a spell in Australia, he arrived in France, where he was exposed to the national classics of Emile Zola, Victor Hugo and Honoré de Balzac. Eventually, the path led to Hugo's *The Hunchback of Notre Dame*, banned from the school syllabus for its adult content (particularly the lust-driven misadventures of corrupt priest Claude Frollo). The book blew his mind, as did another distinctly off-curriculum work *Romeo and Juliet*. Both would end up being adapted into disco concept albums that continue to puzzle and delight aficionados. Although neither gained anywhere near the popularity of *Jeff Wayne's Musical Version of The War of The Worlds*, they received heavy DJ play in their respective years, particularly *Romeo and Juliet's* first side. Aletti loved Costandinos for pushing European disco ahead— "experimenting with the narrative structure, intensifying the movement and thematic flow of the music" and the detailed arrangements kept the Eurodisco style from "threatening to wear thin." Meanwhile, there was the exceptionally high quality of the audio, which came down to the recently installed forty-eight-track recording facility at London's Trident Studios, where Costandinos preferred to record. *Romeo and Juliet,* noted by Aletti as a musical peak of the subgenre, was among the first albums to be recorded there. He also praised his *Hunchback* for its "thrilling, brilliantly crafted, precise yet emotionally rich" music. Yet thesame" album demonstrated the problems involved in attempting storytelling through disco: the dramatic exposition had a tendency to keep interrupting the flow of musical movement.

This wasn't such an issue when the music was primarily destined for home listening. *War of the Worlds* had an open relationship with the dancefloor, with one of its tracks "The Eve of the War" spun off and remixed for disco play. However, its long passages of Richard Burton's narration—often over ambient soundscapes—turned it into something between rock opera and audiobook with a beat. When the concept album was based completely in disco, a conundrum became apparent. Some producers had lofty ideas about adapting well-known stories (or creating their own original ones) into the medium of a disco album. But who wanted to pay attention to narration and dialogue in the middle of a night out dancing? The two simply didn't fit together. The limitations of disco as a long-form narrative medium obviously hadn't occurred to Costandinos, who forged ahead with grandiose plans for a cycle of concept albums. In early 1978, he told Aletti he was planning the first of a projected 12-album interpretation of the *Arabian Nights*. With disco's demise on the horizon, there was little chance that the saga, to be spread over two years of releases, would ever get finished. In fact, it was never even started. At least Costandinos couldn't be faulted for quality control and the kind of ambition that some other producers sorely lacked. Another fairy-tale "adaptation," Russian-born Boris Midney's disco version of *Pinocchio*, came out under the name of his female studio group Masquerade. One of its malformed nuggets "Don't Keep Me Hanging" contains the immortal line "I feel like a puppet, you make me a clown . . . let's get down!" Finely crafted storytelling, it was not.

How, then, did *Once Upon A Time* manage to get it so right? Moroder/Bellotte/Summer at least had a head start on the art. Before she finally emerged as a disco artist, the budding team spent two years making pop/rock story songs that Summer aptly summarized later as "a bit melodramatic with a tilt toward the schlocky side of life." The "gift" of being able to tell stories as a singer-*songwriter*, proclaimed in her autobiography *Ordinary Girl* was slow to develop, but as a *singer*, at least, Moroder and Bellotte provided her with a strong early start. In "The Hostage," she sang the role of the wife of a kidnapped husband in a lurid saga of a botched ransom payment. At the end of the song, she intones "well . . . they found my husband a few days later" in a campy sad voice that echoed the pocket melodramas of The Shangri-Las. If the song wasn't quite up to the Shangri-La's gold standard, it brought Summer her first big hit, at least in The Netherlands and Belgium, where it unexpectedly topped the charts. Although largely ignored today, the recordings were vital in developing the fruitful working relationship between the three, bringing together Moroder's time spent making *Schlager* (a catchy kind of continental pop music) with his new *protégée's* experience in musical theatre.

Originally, Summer's sights were set firmly on an acting career, but she quickly and astutely realized that opportunities would be limited for an aspiring black actress at that time. Singing was a more established pathway to success for black women, and, she intuited, would prise open the right doors. After her pop career flourished, she made some overtures towards acting again and gained exposure in the disco film *Thank God It's Friday*, the would-be rival to *Saturday Night Fever* produced by Casablanca Filmworks, (a movie-making subsidiary of her record label Casablanca). However, it proved to be a disappointment to her. She clinched the climactic moment of the film, and her performance of "Last Dance" provided her not just with a huge hit, but both the Golden Globe and Academy Award for best song in 1978. Frustratingly, though, the film was a hollow showcase for her other talents with "virtually no acting required" and led to no further film roles. Much of this energy ended up being channeled into her artful approach to singing and writing. She preferred creating characters to "personalized songwriting," as the latter was simply too painful for a singer with an often-turbulent personal life. Giving voice to the character in a song was an art Summer felt she approached "as an actress approaches a script" and Bellotte recalls that as a singer, she was a "natural" who was adept at trying on new voices. Just because she felt like it, she might arrive in the studio and sing high "like Mickey Mouse," even as Bellotte chided her for being too extreme. If she sometimes went too far, the zeal for vocal experimentation helped to bring a texture to her characterization in *Once Upon A Time* that few pop albums have achieved since.

Bellotte also happened to be another member of the team with a long-standing interest in story. Despite being immersed in the German culture of his Munich home, he still kept up a lifelong passion for English literature by voraciously reading his way through the shelf of grey-spined *Penguin Classics* that he found in his local store (named "English Books"). The three novels of Mervyn Peake's *Gormenghast* series were favorites that sparked the idea of writing a triptych of interlocking songs. The resulting three-songs-in-one ("Try Me," "I Know" and "We Can Make It") finally combined to make a fourth composite song "Try Me, I Know We Can

Make It," filling Side 1 of *Love To Love You Baby's* follow-up album *A Love Trilogy*. At first, the connection between music and literature didn't go much further than basic numerology. In Summer's next album, released eight months later, Bellotte expanded his reach and created a full song cycle (another structure borrowed from classical music). *Four Seasons of Love* took its primary inspiration, not from the famous Vivaldi concerti, but another sequence of novels, Laurence Durrell's *The Alexandra Quartet*. Something of an overlooked gem, at just over thirty-two minutes, *Four Seasons of Love* is Summer's shortest album and, as with its predecessor, by modern standards the four songs look like an EP at best. Nevertheless, it can lay claim to a first in disco—organizing an entire two sides of music around a focused, unified theme. Arguably, it was the first *proper* disco concept album. If the album struggled to produce hits, its ambition didn't go unnoticed. A *Billboard* article by Radcliffe Joe cited it as evidence that disco was "undergoing subtle, but distinct changes in lyric and rhythm content." As formulaic disco records flooded onto the market that were dismissed as "mindless and insulting to the intelligence of audiences," many were looking for evidence that record labels, producers and artists were aiming for something more sophisticated. Donna Summer's twice-yearly album releases seemed to offer a way out. With Bellotte's next literary inspiration, he went deeper and longer with the twelve-novel series by Anthony Powell—*A Dance to the Music of Time*. As the series progressed, the novels, an examination of English political and cultural life in the mid-twentieth century, worked their way from the early 1920s through to the present of the 1970s. Once again, Bellotte took the structuring principle rather than the theme of his literary inspiration and applied it to his album-craft. *I Remember Yesterday* opens in a similar era to the novels with the charleston-styled disco of the title track. The two sides then work their way through subsequent decades of pop music, settling in the disco present before the final track "I Feel Love" fast-forwards into the future, unwittingly altering the course of electronic music along the way.

As a double album, *Once Upon A Time* took on a different principle in its structure. As if it were a stage musical or "disco opera" (as Christgau understood it), the four sides were now described as "acts." Each one of the acts is fairly self-contained and, in its own way, aims at some kind of sonic cohesion. There's also a point of story tension at the end of each side, like a cliffhanger but less dramatic, that encourages attentive listeners to keep going further and flip the record. There's a story to be explored of how Summer tried to adapt the album into a piece of real musical theatre, but it's elusive—little detail was ever discussed. In interviews she gave to promote *Once Upon A Time* in late 1977, she first revealed how plans were being hatched for a September 1978 debut in Boston or Philadelphia. Eventually, she hoped, it would transfer to New York. As she continued thinking about the project during 1978, it got a name—*Cindy* and was even registered in early 1978 in U.S. copyright records. The records make the musical look like a serious proposition, but tell us little more than we already know—"*Cindy:* a love story/concept and story by Donna Summer, Joyce Bogart, Susan Munao; treatment written by Joyce Bogart." In her *Penthouse* interview in July 1979, she was still apparently "considering" the project. However, Pete Bellotte remembers it as "just an idea" that clearly fell by the wayside—a victim, perhaps, of Summer's burgeoning success in other areas. She confessed in interviews that she was actually "more into Broadway than recording," suggesting that she may have been looking to *Cindy* for a way out from her fast-rising pop career. "Whether it's a flop or a success doesn't matter," she added, "what matters is that I tried." Until the more recent run of jukebox musicals kicked off in the 1990s, disco didn't have much luck on the stage anyway. An earlier "disco-rock ballet" *Street Talk*, written and masterminded by Four Seasons songwriter Bob Crewe in 1976 also failed to make it to Broadway, although it, too, left behind an ambitious and expensively recorded concept album.[4] By the end of 1978, Summer had moved back definitively into recording, creating what would be her biggest success: the *Bad Girls* album. She would never make another serious attempt to break into the acting world again.[5]

Years after its release in 1982, Summer told the NME's Barney Hoskyns she felt it was "structurally the best album I've ever recorded," although what she meant by that deserves some exploration. Continuity is important in extended-form disco—it needs similar mood, orchestration, style and, particularly, tempo to keep the dancing flowing. But there

[4] The one that finally got to Broadway—the critically panned *Got Tu Go Disco*, starring a young Irene Cara in 1979—closed after just nine performances.
[5] In 1979, she told the *New York Times'* John Rockwell that she still wanted to "do movies" and was looking at "14 different scripts, but so far I haven't found the right thing." Evidently, the right thing never came up.

also has to be enough variation to keep the listener actively engaged. Achieving a golden balance between the two across an entire double album was no mean feat, and something nobody had attempted before. *Once Upon A Time* is complex but uses some simple methods to keep the music coherent across its sixteen tracks. Half of these are in a home key of A minor, which is introduced in the opening title track and then present on every one of its sides. The reprises of the title track are another tried-and-tested trick to keep the listener keyed in to the musical progression of the story, and bring us back continually to the key emotion in the title track—longing. Unsurprisingly for disco, tempo is a crucial factor, and three of the suites are regulated strictly to the same one. Giving each side a stronger identity, the use of tempo helps break down a large amount of material into more digestible units—sixteen tracks into four. But in case the same-tempo regime was threatening to become predictable, the third side breaks dynamically from it, injecting a range of styles and tempos at just the right point (as well as beginning in a different key). Those are the basics, and the rest is down to detail and the careful manipulation of mood and style that often happens late in the recording process. *Once Upon A Time* achieves this though its group effort—the individual contributions of the collaborators on the album all leave their mark, ensuring that there is enough light and shade along the way to prevent the music slipping into formula.

Let's now compare *Once Upon A Time* to another discopop narrative set in a disco—Barry Manilow's "Copacabana (At the Copa)." "Copacabana" is so dense in narrative information that an entire TV film was eventually spun out of it in 1985, elaborating on the saga of Tony, Rico and Lola across ninety-six minutes instead of four. It finally succeeded where *Once Upon A Time* had failed–becoming a full-length two-act stage musical in 1994. If Manilow's song manages to encapsulate the story in a few minutes, it's only because it cleaves to a strict pop structure of verse/chorus, as do other disco pocket narratives like Boney M.'s "Rasputin." "Copacabana" lacks the basic stages of beginning, build-up and catharsis that makes the best examples like Costandinos' epics, and its lyrical content is shunted out of the way to the beginnings and ends, so narratively compelling. Over four sides, *Once Upon A Time* has room to expand, and there's no need to cramp story inside any individual song. At an average of over four-and-a-half minutes, there's plenty of scope for each track to stretch out and be far more free in its internal structure (perhaps this is what Summer was *really* talking about in her comments on structure). Crucially, the songs don't have the burden of having to deliver a lot of story detail and can simply freeze-frame a mood, emotion or scenario. The title of "Happily Ever After," for example, says pretty much everything you need to know about the song. But there's one exception.

As the opening song, and prologue, the title track of the album does exactly the opposite. It's tasked with packing enough exposition into its three verses to kick off the story with real pace and without it, we might be stuck in the old paradigm of the concept album that "needs explaining." Frantically multi-tasking, the song has to set the emotional tone (melodramatic with a *soupçon* of tragedy) and the key (quite literally) for the entire album, while telling us everything we need to know about its protagonist in just three verses. In doing so, it breaks a few protocols that the other songs on the album have to follow. Tellingly, it's the only song lyric that comes purely in third, as opposed to first person, which undoubtedly helps with the thrifty storytelling. This technique was also used by Disney, whose prologues, visualized as the turning pages of a storybook, begin many of their animated fairy tales. As an album starter, "Once Upon A Time" manages to be memorable through sheer bombast and drama, providing emotional shock and awe instead of the comfortingly gloopy choirs that open Disney's early fairytales. The arranger Bob Esty throws all the musicians at his disposal at the song's arrangement—*tutti* dynamics that are more akin to Tchaikovsky's *1812 Overture* than the gentle prelude to a Wagnerian opera.

It's probably the strong dynamics that encouraged Casablanca to try it out as the album's third single in Japan and a few other European territories (France, Spain, Sweden). Although the song got some decent disco play (the whole of Side A was popular with DJs at the time), "Once Upon A Time," was never very likely to become a hit. It certainly isn't lacking in the deliciously camp histrionics that made "I Will Survive" and Three Degrees "Givin' Up Givin' In" so beloved of the gay audience. But perhaps it doesn't work so well as a single, because the story is convoluted and it's impossible to immediately identify the *cause* of the melodrama. It's an introduction to the singer, rather than a rounded story, and the three carefully staged verses each reveal different aspects of the character and how she feels about her life. The information is all essential, but only for understanding what's to come: the opening verse explores the extent of her interiority, and establishes that she is an arch fantasist and damaged individual (with "hiding from reality" the key phrase). Verse 2 quickly shifts focus and presents the facts of her social isolation: the family that exists in name alone; the wider inability to connect to the people around her. Without it, we may wonder why there are no other characters presented in the album. The third verse is more hopeful, identifying a potential escape from her dire situation—that one day a man might come to lift her out of her loneliness. It's optimistic, but not the triumphant full-voice optimistic of a Disney "I Want" song (The Hunchback of Notre Dame's "Out There," for example). What is lyrically the most upbeat verse plays against expectation musically, by taking it down to a whisper and thinning out the arrangement to a skeleton. Rather than point towards the womanliness she might possess in the future, the voice here is of a little girl. For all her elaborate dreaming, she's uncertain, broken almost.

In all its grandiosity, the title track betrays an ambition—a need, even—to grasp the story by the horns, and with it pull you into the grotto of its fairy tale world. Overblown with its massed choirs, it attempts to reach past anything disco had done before, but is also immaculately assembled and precise. As the curtain opens on the show, we get what is perhaps some of the purest kind of European disco. Under the glitter ball we gather, as romance and drama reach back into the past. *Once Upon A Time* has begun.

## 2
## Faster and Faster to Nowhere:
## Fairy Tales and the Black
## Urban Experience

*Once Upon A Time, on the eve of the new year, a baby girl arrived into the world. She was named LaDonna Adrian Gaines and one day she would grow up to become the star Donna Summer. However, her first few years were spent in the humblest surroundings—a poor housing project in Boston. When Donna turned six, her family moved to a bigger house on the edge of the city. The new neighborhood was middle-class and "partially integrated" (which meant that if you were a black family trying to fit in, you'd better be on your best behavior, in case the neighbors pointed their fingers). On one floor of the house lived her aunt, uncles and cousins and on another her grandmother and even more cousins. There were so many cousins, Donna couldn't even count them on her fingers! It was hard to get a moment's silence in the house and if you wanted your voice heard, you had to talk VERY loud. Some days, with so many people bustling around, Donna went to sit quietly in a closet alone. If she couldn't escape at home, she thought, at least she could daydream herself away to somewhere else. Every Sunday, the family went to a church where everybody sang. When Donna stood up to sing, to her surprise she discovered that everybody wanted to listen. Somehow, she knew that she was very special and that God had great plans for her.*

*When the girl turned nineteen, the time arrived to leave for the big city—the place where her dreams could finally come true. Her mother and father fretted about their young daughter going to New York, which in those days was a VERY dangerous place. Walking one evening, Donna strayed from the path and found herself lost in a strange neighborhood called The Bowery. Suddenly, a strange man emerged from the shadows. Although he was dressed in rags, his face shone with a bright light. To Donna's astonishment he had a message for her. "Soon you will meet a man!" he said. "He will give you a test—you will pass it and receive the opportunity to cross the waters!" Donna went home and puzzled over his words—what could they mean? Later the same day, while singing in her room as usual, she heard knocking at the door. To her further astonishment, she found a second man standing there. He asked Donna to audition to be the singer in his show. What's more, the show, called* Hair, *was travelling to Europe—across the waters![1] Donna knew all about* Hair *and she had always dreamed of going to Europe. This was it—the golden chance from the man's prophecy! Her destiny had called, and the journey had just begun.*

---

[1] The man was Broadway producer Bertrand Castelli, who offered her a choice of the new productions in England, France, or Germany.

The story above may be a "fairy tale," but none of the events within it are fictional. Instead, they're distilled from *Ordinary Girl: The Journey*, the memoir Donna Summer published eight years before her death in 2004. As such we might take the events to be true, although it's worth bearing in mind the tendency of stars to mythologize how they became stars in the first place. Myth-making plays a vital role in creating their public image, but the process must be deeply personal to them as well. How did I get here? Why was it *me* this happened to? In making sense of her often tortuous path through the trials of stardom, Summer glossed each twist and turn with a magical significance— fate, augers and even the intervention of guardian angels were all credited with shaping her life story. For the cynic, her interpretations often raise eyebrows, and her world view was clearly influenced by the mysticism percolating through the post-hippy culture that was the backdrop to her rise to fame. God was also credited with shaping events, which all became post-rationalized within her deep Christian belief system, and she mentions "God's plan" more than once. It might seem disingenuous, silly even, to rewrite the events in her life in the form of a fairy tale. Yet it was the singer herself who repeatedly affirmed how she saw her life *as* a fairy tale. The experience of living in Germany became at least a chapter is this, and she recalled a snowy stay under the fairytale castle of Neuschwanstein (Disney's inspiration for the Sleeping Beauty castle) with the misty-eyed verve of an emigrant from the New World. But the fairy story ran deeper. During and after the promotion for *Once Upon A Time*, she confessed how she felt like a "modern-day Cinderella" and that the album was her "life story in reality." The story seemed so real to her, she claimed, that during the recording process she was often moved to tears. In another interview she claimed it was "the first record I can really say is a part of me." Moroder had an additional take, observing from the sidelines of the studio that what was coming out in the record was ten years of hard graft, taking in the additional pressures of "a very hard life with her daughter." It's not difficult to pick holes and point out the many areas where her actual life story deviated from the musical fairy tale. The young singer hadn't escaped a home life of neglect and abuse, for example. Quite the opposite, her extended family growing up was as warm and loving as could possibly be imagined. Still, like Diana Ross a decade earlier, her rise from the projects to become one of the biggest singers of her era was something a young black girl could scarcely dream of. Could young black girls even become princesses? There were, and largely still are, scarce examples for a young child to look up to. This is a vacuum that the big entertainment companies like Walt Disney, who have positioned themselves as the principal gatekeepers of "princess culture," have struggled to address. As co-written and sung by a black woman, *Once Upon A Time* has a role to play in shaping this culture, although the concept for an album with a fairy tale theme wasn't hers in the first place. Bellotte remembers receiving a brief direct from her record label Casablanca, who demanded "another themed album, this one to be a fairy story, a modern Cinderella," something involving a prince. Where this seed idea originated is stated more clearly on the album cover, coming not from

Casablanca's flamboyant record label boss Neil Bogart,[2] but his father Al Bogatz, who had written songs for his budding pop star son (then "Neil Scott") at the tail end of the 1950s. Before long, Summer was involved in an intense process of story devising with co-managers Joyce Bogart (wife of Neil) and Susan Munao in Los Angeles, and together they expanded on the initial concept. Although not her idea to begin with, after receiving the brief she embraced the concept, inhabited it fully, and entwined the story with her own.

In rewriting the Cinderella story to suit her own ends, she wasn't exactly lacking material to draw on. Of all the fairy tales, Cinderella is the most adapted by a long chalk. It has inspired operas and ballets since the late eighteenth century as well as being present at the very early days of cinema, thanks to French pioneer George Melies' 1899 silent short. More than any other fairy tale, writers seem compelled to turn it into a musical, with new versions for stage, television and film produced in virtually every decade. There's a certain logic within this—the central scene is, of course musical in nature. The grand ball has been accompanied over the centuries by everything from eighteenth-century French courtly dance to waltz, jive and, of course, disco. As the decades pass, other musical conventions have also crept in. There's often, for example, a "wishing" song early in the story, and a more whimsical fairy godmother song around the key

---

[2] In case you're wondering, Bogart renamed himself (as well as his record label Casablanca) in homage to Humphrey Bogart, the star of his favorite film.

transformation sequence. Like any fairy tale, Cinderella is a psycho-spiritual journey with deep cultural roots. Carl Jung understood fairy tales as expressions of the collective unconscious, a storehouse of collective wisdom from which all human mythology derives. Swirling within this primordial soup of motifs and images are the common elements from which all Cinderella stories are formed. These include basic human characteristics like goodness, envy, and cruelty, which are global rather than restricted to one ethnic group. Although Cinderella herself is European (the origins of her name are in the Neapolitan variant *Cenerentola* by Giambattista Basile, from the Italian word for ashes, *cenere*), the Cinderella-type tale is found in almost every continent around the world, particularly Europe and Asia. Cinderella variants told from the black perspective (African, Caribbean and African American) are less common, but there are enough for Deborah L. Thompson's article "Not All Cinderellas Wear Glass Slippers" to be able to compile a useful list of them. Look at some of their titles, and they aren't immediately recognizable as Cinderella tales. In *Nomi and the Magic Fish* and *The Ox of the Wonderful Horns* (South African variants from the Zulu and Xhosa groups), castles, balls and coachmen don't figure large, which is understandable given their places of origin. Read further, though, and familiar motifs emerge: cruel stepmothers, unkind siblings, tasks to perform, magical helpers and, of course, some kind of transformation. The central character within these is an idea in flux and constantly in reinvention across time and space. In the West, Cinderella is most familiar as a kind, compassionate figure and in the German version from the Brothers Grimm (whose good girls and women are generally silent), she plays according to type. Travel just a few hundred miles away and a Czech film from 1973 *Three Wishes for Cinderella* portrays her as an impish and flirtatious trickster who steals the prince's horse and mocks him from high up in a tree. Cinderella, then, is not one girl, but a legion of them and, sometimes, is even a boy, like Babette Cole's *Prince Cinders*. The more you look for Cinderellas, the more you find; and disco, it turns out, is full of them. What could be more Cinderella-like than Italian–American Tony Manero trying to rise out of the dead-end New York suburbs of *Saturday Night Fever* and going to the ball in his own peacocking style.

Since 1950, there has been one major threat to all this rich variety—the might of the Walt Disney Company. After *Snow White and the Seven Dwarfs* in 1939, *Cinderella* became their second animated feature-length fairy tale, and many of its cues are taken from the most popular printed version–that written in the late seventeenth century by Frenchman Charles Perrault. Perrault's Cinderella may have introduced the fairy godmother, pumpkin, and glass slippers, but it was the globalizing power of Disney that imprinted these motifs on the mass consciousness as the definitive Cinderella. Almost no discussion of post-1950 Cinderella is possible without considering the Disney effect, such is the entertainment giant's talent for colonizing global cultural heritage and branding it as its own. This is as much true for *Once Upon A Time* as anything else, and it's in the packaging where the Disneyfication is most obvious. With a combination of powder blue background and ivory dress, the outer sleeve emulates the signature colors of the 1950 Disney film. The gatefold inner sleeve riffs on Disney even harder—Summer's giantess sowing magical star seeds over Manhattan alludes to the famous "pixie dust" effect, first developed for the slow-falling shower of sparkles that settles over Cinderella's dress during her transformation scene.[3] Subsequently reused for *Peter Pan's* Tinkerbell and many other fairy tales, it ended up as an integral part of Disney branding, now instantly familiar from the Sleeping Beauty Castle logo that appears before their content. The image of Summer on the inner sleeve may have taken inspiration from Disney, but it was so striking and original in itself that Michael Jackson pinched the idea lock stock and barrel for a sequence in The Jackson's effects-laden "Can You Feel It" video (if you don't believe me, fire it up on YouTube).

There's another consequence to the Disney homage on the sleeve, though. Disney may have got a *lot* better in recent years in addressing representation in their output, but in 1977 the levels of diversity that audiences now enjoy were still a distant dream. Whether deliberate or not, the creeping references to Disney in the sleeve arguably put a frame of whiteness around the Donna Summer project. Is this a big issue within the *Once Upon A Time*? It *could* lay claim (just) to being the first "black" adaptation of the European story variant (if not the first black Cinderella story-type), but it's questionable whether it's actually trying to. Does it become a

---

[3] There's a useful explanation of the effect in an online video essay by one of Disney's veteran animation designers Marlon West, where he demonstrates its use across several films.

"black adaptation" simply because the music and story were presented by a black singer? Some songs are obviously steeped in black performativity ("If You Got It, Flaunt It" comes quickly to mind) but many others (like "Working the Midnight Shift") really aren't. Overall, the album doesn't participate strongly in the Afrocentricity that other black performers were engaged with in the same decade. Perhaps we should stick to thinking of it as not a black but a *disco* adaptation. Even then, the album refuses to settle in disco formula and seems intent on broadening disco's horizons way beyond its R&B origins. Partly, this was down to its producers but also to Summer, who was in the process of trying to expand her audience from its core of black and/or gay disco fans.

Whatever we make of *Once Upon A Time* it's clear, looking back at 1977, that the idea of an unequivocally black adaptation of Cinderella was somehow tangibly in the air. It was on the small screen that it happened first. Within just a few months of Summer's album release, a new TV film appeared on American screens with an entirely black cast. Just like Summer's proposed stage musical, it was called *Cindy,* but it certainly didn't tiptoe around the issue of race. Set in wartime, jazz-age Harlem, the show delighted in broad characterization and ribald dialog that signified blackness heavily, although ironically, none of the writers (*The Mary Tyler Moore Show* and *Taxi* among their credits) were black themselves. This Cinderella, a motherless migrant from South Carolina, is introduced by her father as "a wonderful girl," who makes her step-sisters "look like dog meat." Way beyond the "pert and feisty" Cinderella-type, she is in another category entirely; after first running into her sisters at a rope-jumping contest, she's soon throwing a can of garbage over them. The film is heavy in pantomime and delights in flipping the script at every turn on well-known characters from the original story. The father isn't dead in this take, but a restroom attendant hen-pecked by his new wife; the wife isn't cruel, but possessed of a brusquely pragmatic approach to family; the fairy godmother is a draft-dodging (male) chauffeur, and the prince a vain and grandstanding war hero. The original musical numbers might have been of mixed quality, but the film hits a home run when a cheap gumshoe trawls around with Cindy's soiled white sneaker to see which ball-guest it fits. The choice of soundtrack for the scene—Fats Waller's "Your Feet's Too Big"—is a stroke of pure inspiration. The film is still beloved among those in the black community who remember seeing the original transmission, but there's still an underlying unease that the black girls in the story don't get full access to the full princess fantasy. Ok, so every character is given some kind of happy-ever-after at the end—the ugly sisters wind up as wrestling champions—but nobody really ascends in status. The moral in the final song teaches that love is the secret potion that "makes this dusty old world shine like a jewel" and Cindy's main reward is the joy of motherhood in a tenement block. "Find joy where you can," really isn't such a bad philosophical framework for life, but another way of looking at it is "know your place"—a moral fundamentally at odds with what Cinderella is really about.

There's a reason why the story remains so popular around the world—poor girls are offered hope, however unrealistic, of an uplift in social status. How they get there is up to the writer. The wholesome message of Charles Perrault's version is that personal goodness and virtue eventually win the day, but what really gives the fantasy its potency is the promise of a better future.[4] The fixation on finding a man in *Once Upon A Time* might now seem out of step with contemporary attitudes, but it does at least encourage full participation *in* the fantasy. Finding the right balance in a princess story is no easy task. When Disney, attempting greater inclusivity, eventually created their first African-American princess in 2009's *The Princess and the Frog*, they famously hit speed bumps. Set in the American Deep South, the film was already in trouble during development when the name they had planned for its princess leaked. "Maddie," as she was originally called, caused a firestorm of controversy for its connotations of slavery, and ended up being changed to the more neutral "Tiana." As Disney's first black animated lead, there were also questions about her visibility—for most of the film she wasn't black, but frog-green. Then there was the way the film conveniently papered over the social realities of the time. At the end, the ambitious Tiana gets the restaurant she's been obsessively working towards, but the meritocratic society in which this could happen looked nothing like actual racial history. It seemed Disney couldn't win whatever they tried. Earlier in

---

[4] Perrault's version isn't particularly hopeful on the subject of class. When he wrote his book, rising levels of literacy in Europe meant that the story could be spread to a broad section of the population. However, the second moral at the end of his story, that godmothers are indispensable "for your advancement," was fundamentally elitist—in the late seventeenth century, godfathers and mothers could only be accessed by the wealthy.

1997, a TV remake of the Rodgers and Hammerstein 1957 *Cinderella* musical negotiated a different route around the problem—it used a post-racial rainbow-colored fantasy as a means to side-step race relations entirely. Their Cinders (played by R&B starlet Brandy) is placed in a mixed-race family with both black and white step-sisters; Whoopi Goldberg and Victor Garber were cast as as the queen and king, with Filipino actor Paulo Montalbán as their son. The casting was valiantly unconventional, short-circuiting any preconceptions the audience may have had about ethnic plausibility. If you want to enjoy the fantasy of the movie, which most did, the only way is to leave that particular set of logic behind as yesterday's baggage (the *Variety* review advised viewers to "check your disbelief at the door"). There's a reason, though, why few of the complexities of racial representation affect *Once Upon A Time*—aside from the backing vocalists, there's only a single character running the show.

Pop artists being pop artists, this is generally the norm. Listen to any narrative concept albums where only one singer attempts to inhabit the perspectives of various different characters. They're rarely very effective, as singers are limited to their vocal range and style (see Nine Inch Nails *Year Zero,* where Trent Reznor sounds uniformly like Trent Reznor for evidence). Donna Summer had an advantage here—thanks to her acting background, her vocal armory was remarkably versatile. It allowed her to project many different moods and facets of character ("as many different voices as the producers have styles," was how Aletti put it), but even she didn't attempt to deviate from her character and populate her album with a whole cast. With no record of what Summer had in mind for the stage musical she was planning throughout 1978, it's tempting to speculate about how it would have been executed. A one-woman show with herself in the title role might have been an opportunity to squeeze more juice out of her musical theater background, although with her career about to blow up around the world, perhaps the plan was for another singer to take the part. Adapting the musical to fit a bigger cast of supporting characters seems far more unlikely, as the extra song material needed to make it work would have been so extensive as to dilute the original album. There is an advantage to the one-singer/one-role approach in *Once Upon A Time*— we get a truly nuanced character study from a performer who is up to the challenge. The downside is that we miss out on the viewpoints of the wider Cinderella cast. There's no *deus ex machina* role here for a fairy godmother and no ugly sisters. Even more unusually, in a tale at its core about the relationships between children and abusive or neglectful parents, there's a big hole where parents should be. To go looking for an obvious villain in the piece—some wicked queen or impish magical tormentor—is also to head for disappointment. But that isn't to say there are no antagonists at all. Where we might expect ugly sisters, Cinderella instead has to run a gauntlet of indifferent city dwellers and cut-throat disco divas. Standing in for the oppressive wicked stepparent are threats of social isolation, exploitative labor or even violence in an unforgiving urban society. Finally, with no fairy godmother around to lend a helping wand, if she wants to create a suitable exterior for the world, the only person the heroine can rely on is herself. In this version of the story (the *truly* American one?) only hard work and ambition will get you to the ball. The shift towards contemporary urban realism has one other significant effect—out of the window goes conventional magic, wands, coachmen-mice and all. In fact, the closer you peer at it, the less *Once Upon A Time* looks like a traditional Cinderella.

While we're picking holes, let's discuss the elephant in the ballroom: feminism. In the 1998 Cinderella movie *Ever After*, Drew Barrymore's heroine, Danielle, might dwell in the fifteenth century, but she spouts economic theory and debates the ethics of land-owning with the Crown Prince before she finally marries him. Meanwhile, in *Once Upon A Time*, Donna Summer's character is fixated with snagging a man and making herself pretty: the only thing she can think of to achieve her dream. The way she tries to fit into the world isn't exactly progressive nor is there any open critique of her methods within the songs. It's almost as if (gasp) she's never even heard of second-wave feminism. Media scholars categorize fairy tale retellings into two different groups, and through her actions, she falls into one of them. The first of these is termed *duplicates*, for how fairy-tale codes from past eras are repeated with all their problematic sexist and social stereotyping intact. The other *revisionist* group does the opposite, setting out deliberately to alter the traditional codes, images, or social relationships within the original fairy tales. As these codes are mostly hangovers from the feudal period, writers understandably want to keep them where they belong, hopefully subverting the views of readers as they go along.

While they undoubtedly still have their charms, early Disney films like *Snow White & The Seven Dwarfs* and *Cinderella* are often problematized as belonging in the first group. So, by and large, does *Once Upon A Time*. At the end of the story the girl rides off into the sunset with a man she seems to barely know, and few lessons learned about herself. If we found out more about the man's personal qualities, perhaps this ending would be easier to swallow. Really, though, the prince is a blank cipher. He's little different from the one in Disney's *Snow White* (who doesn't even have a name in the film, by the way) and as a romantic foil, he's as *duplicate* as you could imagine. Why should we expect anything different in a disco album though? Disco is not punk, and the voice of Cinderella isn't being provided by Poly Styrene or Siouxsie Sioux. Systemic inequality, particularly where women was concerned, wasn't exactly in disco's lyrical repertoire. You could point to *Saturday Night Fever* and the dominant role of Stephanie Mangano in her relationship dynamic with Travolta's Tony Manero as evidence of a more progressive discussion around men and women. However, in bringing the fairy tale up to date for the urban late 1970s, it's more the physical setting of *Once Upon A Time* than its social coding that seems "modern." In this, it borrows heavily from Hollywood, whuch for many decades has been upscaling from the small medieval town to the big city of New York in its modern fairy tale adaptations. Why is the Big Apple such an irresistible setting? Probably the main reason is that the directness of the city's inhabitants; its sketchy neighborhoods and grimy streets offer an irresistible counterpoint to the rustic or courtly settings of Europe. This ruse rarely gets tired in cinematic fairy tales and has been exploited in movies from *Splash* to *Pretty Woman* and *Black Swan*. Even Disney tried their hand at it in 2007 in the self-satirical *Enchanted* with its helpful vermin tidying up the messy apartment instead of bluebirds and cute mice in the "Happy Working Song." New York's architecture adds something special in itself—perhaps the immense strangeness of the concrete jungle allows it to stand in for the endless and unfathomable green of European forests.

An urban setting suggests urban music, though, and in 1977, that just about still meant the blaxploitation-era soul that had exerted its own influence on disco (notably The Temptations' loose and cyclical "Law of the Land"). The closest *Once Upon A Time* gets to this in the edgier first two sides of the record is the album's second track "Faster and Faster to Nowhere." A stagey, almost pantomime sketch of a deteriorating urban environment, it cleaves far more closely to Bowie's "1984" (originally written for a stage adaptation of George Orwell's novel) than it does to Stevie Wonder's "Living For The City" or Bobby Womack's "Across 110th Street." The song might be performed by a black woman, but it perplexingly reads better as a white person's hysterical odyssey into a deprived inner-city neighborhood than black protest song. Bowie's track might have borrowed heavily from Isaac Hayes' "Theme from Shaft," but its rock opera sci-fi take on the blaxploitation soundtrack recalibrated the inner city into the dystopian hyper-city of the near future. "Faster and Faster" isn't so much urban realism as hyper-realism, almost expressionist in how it evokes paranoia. The intricate, suffocating wall of sound it conjures renders New York as both oppressive and spectacular. If the opening track was the big introduction to the main character, track 2 provides the introduction to the setting. Having said that, the city feels more like a character than a setting here, a monster chasing the inner-city Cinderella down dark alleys. The exaggerated emotional response in the song became a feature of Summer's live shows, where she embellished it with increasingly dramatic ad-libs on stage ("I can't breathe, I need heeeeeelp" in her 1979 Osaka show is a prime example). After making its presence felt tangibly here, some sense of the city is then sustained musically through much of the rest of the album. It filters through the wee-small-hours blues of "Working the Midnight Shift" to the high-end opulence of "Happily Ever After," always managing to steer tastefully and imaginatively clear of blaxploitation cliché.

If we're looking for inner-city intertexts for the album, the closest isn't another album anyway, but a film contemporary that shared its fairy-tale-in-New York setting. *Once Upon A Time* is strikingly similar in both its setting and central character to *The Wiz*, Sidney Lumet's 1978 all-black musical adaptation of *The Wizard of Oz*. Dorothy, played by Diana Ross in the film, is a shy twenty-four-year old elementary school teacher, reluctant to fly the family nest. The casting was widely regarded as implausible, given Ross' age at the time (thirty-three), but it gave the character an air of eerie perpetual adolescence that, in retrospect, makes the film more interesting. Ross' performance is often criticized for being over the top and relentlessly neurotic—imagine the psychological drama of "Faster and Faster to Nowhere" maintained over an entire movie—but in her paranoia, neediness and apparent difficulties in entering adult life, she's evenly matched with Cinderella in Acts 1 and 2. Aletti even noticed the similarity between the two in the final reprise of the opening title theme, where Summer's "over-dramatic reading" sounded "surprisingly like Diana Ross."

Dorothy's emotional estrangement from her family provides the psycho-dramatic spur that incites a colorful head-trip through the urban Oz, where she lands after the snowstorm that stands in for the original film's tornado. Like Donna Summer's Cinderella, she's introverted to the point of psychological crisis. The arcs for the two characters are uncannily similar—they have both retreated into deep fantasy worlds, from which the challenge is to escape out into the city and eventually prosper. In the case of *The Wiz,* this becomes the vivid, alternate reality of the film, where sets were built over real (but now disappeared) New York landmarks of the time. At certain points, *Once Upon A Time* and *The Wiz,* which has its own disco-inspired ball at the Emerald City,[5] often align so closely that it's hard to believe they were not at least aware of each other's existence. Given the timings of their respective productions, they probably weren't (although it's highly likely that Summer had taken note of the earlier successful stage version).[6] This is corroborated by Bellotte, who has never seen the film himself and confesses no knowledge of any mutual influence.

[5] The Emerald City, in fact a dressed-up World Trade Center Plaza, is the ultimate disco ball in all but name. Over 400 dancers populated the set piece (Lumet claimed it was the largest number ever to appear simultaneously on screen) and the three costume changes for each dancer added up to a staggering 1,200 costumes in a single sequence.

[6] The stage version, originally starring disco star Stephanie Mills, predated the album by three years.

*The Wiz* was expensive—its $23 million budget was, at the time, by far the highest for an all-black production—more than twice the cost of *Star Wars*. When it failed at the box office, it was recognized as bringing to an end a wave of black-cast cinema triggered by the blaxploitation boom, which relied heavily on the support of the American black audience. *The Wiz* arrived at a time of enthusiasm for the black "remake," including 1970s horror knock-offs like *Blackula* and *Blackenstein* and the gangster film *Black Caesar*. Even before she arrived at Cinderella, Donna Summer was already playing an active part in these re-imaginings, restaging well-known white American or European iconography in her own image. Most obviously, you can see this in the sleeve and "calendar" inserts of *Four Seasons of Love,* where she represented each season with a glamour pose alluding to another from the past. On the front cover, she reclines in a suspended half-moon, a popular image dating back to the debut of the Miller High Life "Girl in the Moon," and for "autumn" she famously aped Marilyn Monroe's "flying skirt" scene from *The Seven Year Itch*. Without a doubt, though, the most unusual of the four is "spring" —an intricate homage to Jean-Honoré Fragonard's painting *The Swing*. A visual icon of the Rococo-era with its flower-roped swing and frothy pink dress, the romantic opulence of the image is pure fairy tale.[7] In copying it, Donna

[7] *The Swing* has influenced the look of several fairy tale adaptations, most notably Disney's *Tangled*. In a curious note of cultural alignment, it was also recreated ruffle for ruffle in a musical scene within a *Cinderella* film, *The Slipper and the Rose,* made just as *Four Seasons of Love* was about to go into production.

Summer seemed to be signposting where she would go next in her career.

The same kind of care and attention went into crafting the cover art for *Once Upon A Time,* which according to Bellotte was the most expensive among all of Summer's albums to produce. The cover is unfussy, staged from simple elements, and much of its impact comes from Summer's extraordinary dress. On the rear cover, the giant bat-wing sleeves and high Empire-line bow hang voluminously but architecturally around the body, giving almost the effect of a kimono. With its slightly outlandish boho styling, the image reinvents the Disney Princess for peak-seventies romantic and is quintessentially of its time. The rest of the impact comes from Summer's mesmerizing gaze; the head, as per usual, tilted slightly back. The pose has just-the-suggestion of sexual availability that was a selling point of her record covers throughout the 1970s. In contrast to the sexual ecstasy implied in the *Love to Love You Baby* cover or the more challenging stare-down of the viewer in *Bad Girls,* the gaze into the camera lens for this album is sexually inscrutable, more like a doll than sex siren. Despite the invitation of the gently parted lips, the look in the eyes isn't really seductive— it's blank.[8] Her gaze hovers ambiguously, neither avoiding nor completely meeting the viewer and the overall impression

[8] Unlike her disco-era contemporary Diana Ross, nobody thought to produce a Donna Summer doll during her lifetime, although during the 1980s and 1990s in particular, black fashion dolls—like the Afrocentric Imani— began to look uncannily like Donna Summer herself. Also, watch her 1984 TV performance of "Supernatural Love," where her styling (a fan of back-combed hair and stiff flared party dress) is incredibly doll-like.

is that she is not quite present, disassociating or spun out on Quaaludes.

The inscrutable passivity is acted out in the album's fourth song "Say Something Nice." It sounds as if it was written from a perspective of a needy doll, trying to make her presence felt in the world in a track that brims with thrilling hostility. Between the verse and chorus, violins claw rapaciously over pounding toms at the arrangement, which is much closer to the aggressive environment of "Faster and Faster" than the airy interlude of "Fairy Tale High" that precedes it. In a Norwegian Cinderella variant *Katie Woodencloak*, the Prince is a vicious cad, who calls her an ugly troll and refuses to touch her towel. The threat in "Say Something Nice" isn't that the world is persecuting her, though, there's something far worse—its indifference. In fact, so oblivious is the world to the singer's existence, that she is driven to beg it for compliments. These start off pretty generalized in the first verse ("say that you like me the way I am"), but as the song continues, her need for assurance turns worryingly to the superficial—her appearance. By verse 2, she's become fixated on the trappings of femininity (hair, clothes, and facial beauty) in a case of *like me, like the way I look*. From a contemporary standpoint, it's a message that doesn't flatter the singer; her neediness the negative image of modern female pop. Imagine the unapologetically body-positive Lizzo singing "tell me you think that my hair's real nice" in the key of Summer's insecurity and very 1970s female passivity. It's almost unthinkable. In Jess Glynne's UK hit "I don't wear make-up on Thursday," she at least tries to take control over the pressures to maintain appearance, accepting that the price of occasional loneliness is being able to sit around in sweatpants.

Anyway, it's not as if Summer is trying to provide a role model here for young girls— she's in character, and her character is essentially a troubled one. If you look at the song a different way, there's something about it that, in 1977, seems already to be commenting on the attention-starved economy of the social media-obsessed present. The ingratiating baby talk delivery is deliberately appealing to male attention, but it masks an aggression to which only the backing music gives voice. Until we get to the more impassioned ad libs later on (in a mostly instrumental section) there's little tonal expression to her real feelings. The "you" in the song (which suggests people collectively, rather than any one individual) is never identified, leading to the nagging suspicion, as with so many moments in the album, that the song is another psychodrama playing out in her head. It's one of Summer's more original vocal choices within the album, but it caught some off guard. After he heard a tape of the early sessions for the album, the arranger Bob Esty was surprised enough to question her choices in front of Moroder. What was she trying to achieve on the first two sides? Was she planning to later re-sing the first part and bring the guide up to the "full voice treatment" used on sides 3 and 4? Moroder, knowing her working methods, simply replied that it was already done. In a story that's been repeated by several people who worked on the album, Esty then found himself subjected to a temporary studio ban to keep him out of the way during the recording sessions. Questioning the singer's choices was evidently not part of the remit for an arranger. It was only when he heard the finished album that it finally dawned on him how her unusual styling would fit into the eventual narrative flow. At the end of the day, it seemed Summer had a game plan after all and Esty eventually concluded that she had done a "remarkable job." It's easy to see how he got the wrong end of the stick. Taken on its own, the sickly sweetness of the vocal delivery is a puzzling enough creative decision to take. It's only in the wider album narrative that the juxtapositions with the driving rhythm make sense, and her passive aggression comes into full context.

It was all virgin territory, though. Donna Summer was the first pop star to *really* turn herself into Cinderella and the risk paid off. Perhaps unwittingly, she helped instigate a tradition that would take in countless Cinderella-inspired pop songs and music videos. The possibilities have proven to be endless, from Erykah Badu's Afrocentric *Color Purple*-inspired video for "On and On" to another film musical (still in production at the time of writing) starring Latina pop star Camila Cabello, and featuring a "no gender" fairy godmother played by Billy Porter. In *Once Upon A Time*, Donna Summer may not have made a virtue of her blackness, but the space she opened up for others broadened the scope for who Cinderella could be forever.

# 3
# Working the Midnight Shift—Life and Music Inside the Munich Machine

Some people declare that the world is just a machine.
That there ain't no magic out there.
Never will be, never has been.
— *Cindy, 1978*

*Many years after she arrived in Germany, Donna was living in the Austrian city of Vienna. After arriving in Europe, she'd found great success as an actress and experienced new and exciting things. She wasn't exactly famous yet, but her talent and beauty had brought many admirers. Among them was a golden-haired angel, so Donna thought, called Helmuth. Donna and Helmuth married and soon had a child—a baby girl they named Mimi. But Helmuth, who was himself an actor, was often away working, leaving poor Donna at home looking after the child. Hidden away and lonely, she fell into deep depression. The marriage did not last and before long her dreams of being a singer returned. Just like her strange encounter in New York, fate once again intervened. A friend told Donna about a man looking for singers back in Germany.*

*His name was Giorgio and when he heard her voice, right away he knew its power to tell stories. So began a happy creative partnership. Realizing it was time to become someone new, Donna changed just one letter of her married name, Sommer. Now she was "Donna Summer"—a name fit for a real star.*

*One day the words "I'd love to love you" came to Donna—a new song! When she sang it to Giorgio, he ran around the studio full of ideas. Giorgio turned the lights low and asked Donna to sing very sexily. Lying on the floor, she imagined being someone else, the actress Marilyn Monroe. People loved the song everywhere and back in America, they wanted to hear Donna sing in person. Although Donna wasn't ready, it was time to cross the ocean once again. Just before leaving, she fell deathly ill—her heart was failing her.[1] The doctor told her to keep very still and receive not a single visitor for four weeks. Her body had let her down, and Donna knew deep down that her strong feelings were responsible. Soon she recovered and was ready to go home.*

*Back in America after so many years, everything felt very strange, as if she had never grown up there at all. Even stranger, people imagined that Donna was the sexy woman on her record. Donna was a success, but to keep their fantasy alive, she wasn't even allowed to wear her own clothes outside. Who was she to say no, though? It was as if a great and terrible machine had taken over her life, controlling her every action and thought. Donna wanted so badly to be famous, but the pressures weighed heavily on her. One night, it all became too much. She went to the hotel room window and started to climb over the*

---

[1] The serious problem of myocarditis, an inflammation of the heart muscle.

*railing. One leg in and one leg out, she was ready to throw herself to the ground. But it wasn't yet Donna's time to go. Her leg tangled in a curtain and, try as she might, she couldn't get free. Suddenly a cleaning maid came into the room— how could she explain what she was doing? It was as if, through the curtain and the cleaning maid, God was telling her to stay on earth and continue her life's purpose. But how could she carry on while she was still trapped in the machine?*

"The machine." It was the name Donna Summer gave to the entertainment business complex that conspired, she felt, to commodify her every movement. In an endless litany of "walk this way, talk this way, wear your hair this way, say this, do this, don't say this, don't say that," learning to hold on to her identity—to "the me nobody knows"—was her only defense against its dark arts. The machine may have been her sworn enemy, but it also earned a healthy respect for what it was capable of doing for her. By submitting herself to its relentless motion, suffer though she might, she clearly understood how it would help her achieve her dreams of stardom.[2] In the most celebrated of *Once Upon A Time's* four sides, the machine gets its clearest musical expression in the "electronic" suite on Side 2. Metronomic, synthetic, and in places cold, our journey with Cinderella through her lowest

---

[2] There have long been rumors of a "lost" Donna Summer album from 1976, the planned follow-up to *Love to Love You Baby.* Although there is no verification of its existence, and the rumors largely discredited as a hoax, the album's purported theme (robot sex) and title ("Love Machine") seem to draw on the machine discourse around her work even further.

ebb is painful, even as it manages to be austerely beautiful. As with the *Cindy* television series, *Once Upon A Time* works overtime to mine the magic *within* the machine, spinning precious silver out of late-night misery and exploitation.

After the trials of Side 1, Side 2 opens with a plea for help. "Now I Need You" begins with a machine click (described by Jane Suck as a "typewriter gone spastic"), that exerts a needling pressure on the brain, insistent almost to the point of madness. As this gives way to lightly tripping alternating Moog chords, space opens up in the song to explore an emotional landscape of pain and isolation that's perhaps a more honest expression of the feelings in "Say Something Nice."[3] Replacing the clicks in the rhythm track, a shunting piston takes command and from then on underpins both "Now I Need You" and "Working the Midnight Shift." Tied to the bass kick, the piston wheel turns relentlessly, as the fragile emotions ricochet above it. As with "Say Something Nice," it's never made clear who she is addressing in her plea—friend, parent or former lover, perhaps. Yet there's a wider implication here. Given Summer's own faith, the "you" here can easily also be read as God. If the lyrics don't necessarily support such an interpretation, the music certainly does—an expansive, electro gospel in space, with a choir housed in wide stalls of endless reverb.

What is it that the singer even "needs" anyway? Is she looking for advice? A shoulder to cry on or the "cheer" of a supportive presence? Probably, she doesn't even know herself,

---

[3] If there's a sad feel in the album overall, Bellotte attributes it to the use of the small rather than big Moog synthesizer.

her need a nameless spiritual yearning. Towards the end of the track, the voice disappears and the stage is set for possibly the most poetic sequence of the whole album. In the final minute-and-a-half, the voyage into the emotional cosmos *really* begins, drifting away like a broken satellite into its furthest recesses. With the voice gone, only the spectral residues of the singer's desolation remain, rotating weightlessly beyond the power of any help. It's to my mind the saddest piece of music that Moroder has ever produced, the instrumental epilogue all the more emotionally affecting for its lack of words. In one of the most significant twists on the original Cinderella story, this help never really arrives, the plea remains unanswered. Ultimately, our heroine must go through her trials alone, unsupported by any social or familial networks. Nobody is actually listening; her song just another cry into the wind.

After reaching the lowest ebb in her own personal life, Summer's immediate response to the near-escape from suicide was to start a course of the MAO inhibitor Marplan, which allowed her at least to better function within the work routine. Dramatically increasing her creativity, the drug allowed her to go days at a time without sleep, even if the hyper-functional state was unnerving. With no "shutoff valve," an ambitious and creative mind firing on Marplan was unsustainable, and she soon stopped taking it. Although she implies in her autobiography that life in LA settled down fairly quickly after the turbulence of 1976 when her breakdown occurred, Mikal Gilmore's lengthy *Rolling Stone* piece in early 1978 paints a conflicting portrait. Published just after the release of *Once Upon A Time,* it catches Summer still on the way up the ladder of her success and struggling to keep pace with its demands. Ever the professional, she offered a "detailed, detached explanation" of her tour plans, but the body language Gilmore observed of fraught nerves, tiredness and bloodshot eyes suggested the control was only superficial.[4] Venting about a recent badly organized Italian tour, she confessed "I thought I was going to break. In one airport I was so gone that they had to give me oxygen and wheel me to the plane, and all I could think was 'I've got a show to do tonight.'" Cancelling shows was not an option unless she was "deathly ill." She may have had a tendency towards the dramatic, but the title of her 1980s work anthem, "she works hard for the money" said it all.

Every good story needs a villain, of course, and the machine had become the antagonist in her own life story, a shadowy force that could at least be given a name. *Once Upon A Time* may lack conventional villains, but some of the shapeless villainy of "the machine" seems to have insinuated its way into grooves of the record. The forces that act on the singer throughout the whole album generally aren't individuals, but the infrastructures (economic, social, industrial) that make up society itself. What allows these forces to assume some kind of form is the idea of the city, which effectively becomes a character itself and acts as a proxy for the real people within it (cruel, exploitative, dangerous). By turns marauding ("Faster and Faster to Nowhere"), unsupportive ("Say Something Nice") and unforgiving in its demands for labor ("Working the

---

[4] In other interviews at the time, she recalled even lapsing into speaking German out of pure disorientation.

Midnight Shift"), the city of New York, for that's clearly where we are, is an essential thread in the fabric of the story. The songs may not refer to it directly, but they capture much of what the city was going through at that point in its history. With the effects of a severe fiscal crisis ongoing, the summer of 1977 saw a massive electricity blackout followed by a night of vandalism, looting and arson. Then there was ongoing terror of the Son of Sam murders, adding to the pervading sense of paranoia. The economic crisis and no-go areas are all somehow detectable within the record, housed as they are within the glamour of escapism that disco offered.

The idea that the city can be a character or protagonist has long been around in the study of cinema and literature. From the nineteenth-century Parisian novels of French author Balzac to Woody Allen's *Manhattan* or the 2008 film comedy *In Bruges*, the city often maintains such a charismatic presence in fiction that it can even be considered the star. As the 1970s rolled into the 1980s and then the 1990s, cinematic cities increased in scale, from city to "mega cities" (or *megalopolises* if you like). In movies like *Blade Runner* and *The Fifth Element*, they often became the main draw for audiences. Once this happens, as Thomas Elsaesser's essay on Fritz Lang's silent film *Metropolis* points out, the city as spectacle became the "vanishing point of all contemporary urbanist fantasies of entertainment spaces." These cities were not so much visions of the future as extreme holographic exaggerations of the present, tied to our experiences of modern life. The mega city got its most hypnotic representation in 1984, within the rain-soaked drear of *Blade Runner*; Vangelis' score of burnished synthesizers and sprays of orientalism wouldn't get a separate release for a full twelve years, but it ended up exerting a long influence over the art of the sci-fi soundtrack. It's a shame Moroder's contributions to the way we hear cities in cinema has never been properly examined, but his electronic urbanscapes arrived long before *Blade Runner*. While Kraftwerk fixated on machines and transport in the 1970s, Moroder was exploring cities in many different aspects of his work. It's there in solo album tracks like "Utopia" and "Lost Angeles," for sure. More intriguingly, his fascination also found an outlet in the epic folly of a pyramid-shaped building complex he designed for, but never built, in Dubai.[5] Then there's the "Istanbul Opening" from his score for *Midnight Express* (a surprise Oscar winner in 1979). Reconfiguring the urban soundscape into the science-fiction present, it sets much of the template for Vangelis.

Moroder's pyramid never made it out of the gates of the dream factory, but another of his grand projects did. Encouraged after the success of *Midnight Express* to try rescoring a silent film, it was to the mega city of *Metropolis* that he turned. In 1984, after several years of hard work, he finally completed as full restoration of the film as was possible from the salvaged footage. The new synth-heavy score featuring pop and rock singers of the day spun off hits for Freddie Mercury and Bonnie Tyler but was looked down on by most critics (French critic Brigitte Ceutat archly described it as

---

[5] Spending two years working on the architectural project on in the 1990s, he later rued the time "chasing stupid things." A multimedia exhibition at DUCTAC in Dubai, *Giorgio Moroder's Pyramid* explored the concept of the urban myth that surrounded it, using his music as soundtrack.

*Morodernisé*). Despite this, with the restoration, Moroder had achieved a significant feat of cultural preservation. In sourcing and restoring the incomplete reels of surviving footage into a complete work he managed to bring the film back to popular attention. Largely thanks to Moroder, the influence of *Metropolis* over popular culture since has only broadened. Despite the technical limitations of its time, Fritz Lang's 1927 film makes the city the star as much as *Blade Runner*. The design has informed countless music videos—Queen's "Radio Gaga," Madonna's "Express Yourself," Janet Jackson's "Rhythm Nation" in the 1980s are just the most obvious examples.

A classic "one-percenter" narrative, decades before its time, the film centers on the struggle between an exploited underclass, hidden at the bottom of the city, and a decadent minority living in luxury at the top. Aside from the brilliantly achieved monumental look of the city, the film holds an arguably bigger influence over popular culture in the central character of Maria (played by Brigitte Helm). Maria is a double role—she's not only the wholesome leader of the worker resistance, but also has a sinister robot doppelganger created to spread dissent among the workers. It's this robot version that has been cited (by Elsaesser again) as a "prototype of the female rock star and the pop-performer"; she gets replicated most obviously in the "Queen of the Night" scene in *The Bodyguard*, where a silver-clad Whitney Houston struts in front of video screens loaded with images of *Metropolis*. Not only a post-human but post-gender figure, the robot Maria has also set the template for pop personae from Janelle Monae's ArchAndroid to Beyoncé's Sasha Fierce. It was arguably Summer herself who helped kick off *that* particular trend in live performances of "I Feel Love," where she enacted a peculiar eroticized robo-dance. Tellingly, when he first listened to "Queen for A Day" back in 1978, Mikal Gilmore was reminded of *Metropolis* and its simple maxim "the mediator between the mind and the machine must be the heart." It's a metaphor at which Bellotte also arrived for "I Feel Love": "the machine hammering away underneath, while Donna is the heart." Perhaps in bringing the two together, Summer achieves a synthesis of the two Marias.

The album might have been set in one city, but it was the product of several, including Los Angeles, where it was first conceived. It was in the southern Germany city of Munich, though, that life was breathed into the album. Munich may have been thriving in 1977 but, centuries old and nestled near the foot of the Alps in conservative Bavaria, it was hardly the thrusting megacity of the future. Walking around Munich now, it's hard to imagine that in the 1970s it had become the "new creative hub of Europe," as Summer put it in her autobiography. Signs of its former status as a permissive party town are mostly gone. A recent series of "Freddie Mercury tours" round his old Munich haunts traces the gay subculture that once ruled there, but now only faint echoes of its decadence remain. After the collapse of the Berlin wall, most of its creative community migrated to Germany's new capital, where rents were cheaper and, for those with a pioneering spirit, endless possibilities flowed. Munich, which is among the most expensive German cities to live in, has now settled back into a more dignified cultural slumber.

In 1969, as part of the city's modernization, work was completed on a new building, the Arabella-Hochhaus

(*Hochhaus* meaning "skyscraper") in the east of the city. Its twenty-three floor height is barely imposing for a skyscraper, even by European standards at the time, but the length of 170 meters and floor area of almost 90,000 $m^2$ made it one of the largest European building complexes of its era. To prepare for the Munich Olympics of 1972, part of the building was converted into a hotel to cater for visitors. The rest was retained as apartments and other commercial units, one of which was Moroder's brand new Musicland Studios.[6] The Hochhaus had, and still has despite its age, a reputation for luxury (the upper-floor swimming pool once formed the backdrop for a slinky Boney M. photoshoot). The basement studios were the opposite, known as being cramped and unremarkable in décor.[7] The 24-track facilities at Musicland might not have been able to compare with the larger consoles in other studios like Trident in London, but it still managed to become an important node on the European studio circuit, attracting many of the biggest artists of the decade.

Despite the opulence of the Hochhaus and its facilities, a macabre reputation has grown up around the building, thanks to the high number of people who have used its roof

[6] The building still stands at the time of writing but is scheduled to be demolished (and then rebuilt) in 2026, being ineligible for landmark status. Musicland eventually closed at the start of the 1990s. The reason: the newly built U4 subway runs directly underneath between Arabellapark and Richard Strauss-Straße stations— close enough to cause significant sound interference.

[7] If you want to see evidence, it can be easily observed in the 1985 music video for "One Vision" by Queen, who regularly recorded there.

as jumping off point. Queen's Brian May, well aware of the connection between the suicides and the *Föhn*, a dry-wind weather phenomenon that comes from the nearby Alps, later recalled how Musicland was an "utterly depressing" place to work.[8] The studio that never slept, it ran around the clock to accommodate artists like Bowie and Led Zeppelin, who both preferred working at night, and engineers were often on call 24/7. As producer/songwriters in residence, Moroder and Bellotte produced a remarkable volume of work there, and a core group of musicians ended up being called the "Munich Machine" in response to the industrial quantities of music that poured out of the studios. Just as they had done a decade earlier at Motown (an early inspiration for Moroder), albums rolled smoothly on and off the production line. It's tempting, listening to "Burning the Midnight Oil," a 1978 collaboration between Moroder and singer Chris Bennett, to imagine Moroder himself as the workaholic subject of the song, putting in overlong hours to distract himself from a love affair gone wrong. In fact, the working routine was the opposite. Bellotte and Moroder stuck to a 10–6 routine as regular as any office, and midnight working was strictly prohibited. Being housed inside a hotel complex also meant the convenience of

---

[8] The effects of the *Föhn* are often summoned as evidence for the disturbed moods of Munich dwellers and have been used as a plot device in fiction (causing sleepwalking, murders and other general torment) as well as notorious incidents in real life: Hitler's photographer Heinrich Hoffman wrote that he once tried to soothe the Führer by attributing his bad mood to the wind.

amenities—for lunch, the studio workers would invariably repair to the restaurant upstairs. Bellotte's recollections of his years at Musicland are overridingly positive; he remembers them as a period where "the happiness contributed to the success of the records." Fun was part of the daily routine (Moroder, recording engineer Juergen Koppers, and pianist Keith Forsey are singled out as the biggest jokers) and the constant banter oiled the wheels for the high volume of work.

Although Munich had a growing global reputation as party town, the writer/producer team were impervious to its hedonistic charms. Bellotte "never touched a drink, cigarette or drug in my life" while Moroder was another notorious straight edge. He delighted in the irony of making statements like "I don't even like dancing" and generally only frequented discos when he wanted to check dancefloor reactions to his current demos. With such heavy use of technology, critics presumed that a cold calculation must lie behind his precise methods. In an interview with Moroder in 1979, the NME summed up the media complaints against him as being the man who "almost single-handedly dehumanized disco." Moroder quickly grew tired of defending himself against accusations that his studio methods were eroding the soul from his recordings and started responding to them in his records. For the cover of the debut LP of his Munich Machine studio side project, he commissioned a painting of a pair of dancing robots with lasers shooting from their eyes. With the hindsight of knowing where pop was headed, the image could easily be mistaken as a serious manifesto for its electronic future. In fact, it was a gag, designed to slyly undermine the "inhuman" slights levelled at him.[9] The criticism seems misguided even now, but at the time it proved exasperating. In the same interview, Moroder gave vent to his frustrations: "all this talk of machines and industry make me laugh," he fumed. "Even if you use synthesizers and sequencers and drum machines, you have to set them up, to choose exactly what you are going to make them do." After all, it was hardly as if manipulating the synthesizer was either automatic or a simple task. In Moroder's estimation, it was "at least ten times more difficult" to get good synth sounds compared to an acoustic instrument. "Machinic" became a slight thrown at Eurodisco in general, like Christgau's "fantastic cuckoo clock" jibe about Boney M. Some critics went as far as expressing actual disgust at the way it quantized the soul out of what was, for them, "good, innovative black music, made by blacks" (i.e. R&B-derived disco). "At least the Philly disco records sounded like they were made by humans" complained Nelson George in his 1988 book *The Death of Rhythm and Blues.* Stripped of funk, Eurodisco's rhythms became deracinated, excised from their roots in black music. For George, it made them "perfect for folks with no sense of rhythm." This standpoint held some water—by the end of the 1970s, Middle America had taken the anthems of The Village People to their hearts, giving the white suburban masses something to pump their fists to.

[9] On Munich Machine's next album release, *Whiter Shade of Pale*, the joke was pushed a step further—the credits listed "shop floor, electronics foreman, mechanics foreman, shop steward, apprentice, time and motion study."

In the studio, for Bellotte, the "magic" on the records emerged not from calculation but spontaneity. He would give a chord sheet to the musicians, then play them his demos. After a couple of run-throughs, "one of them, maybe the pianist, would say 'what if I did this?' and you'd say 'oh that's fantastic'. It could sound so different to how it started out, which couldn't really happen so much now." Their approach, in other words, wasn't that different from any 1970s rock band. When *Rolling Stone*'s Dave Marsh later reviewed the 1980 Summer album *The Wanderer*, he read the core team of Summer, Moroder, Bellotte, and Harold Faltermeyer as a collaborative unit that effectively functioned "as a rock band." As disco and rock began to converge towards the end of the 1970s, rock bands like Sparks moved in the other direction; under Moroder's production tutelage, they used disco as a way of disassembling themselves from the passé notion of the "band." Still, there were some basic differences in how a rock band worked and how a Donna Summer dance record was put together, which a rare interview with Bellotte in 1977 clarified. The process would begin with the creation of a guide track on a rhythm machine, the bass and drums would be then recorded over it to create the basic rhythm track. At this point, the arranger (often Bob Esty) would come in to embellish with his own ideas, although much of the arrangement would also happen much later in the mixing stage.

The extent of Bob Esty's role in *Once Upon A Time* has been disputed and, as a fly in the ointment of the story, the account he gives of his own contributions needs some unpicking. As a writer, producer, and arranger he had his own solid involvement in disco, contributing to projects by big names including Cher, Barbara Streisand, and a writing partnership with Paul Jabara, which resulted in Summer's "Last Dance." Esty passed away in 2019, but towards the end of his life he gave several interviews where he discussed *Once Upon A Time.* His account of the writing/recording on the project is at times in stark conflict with Bellotte's. Grand claims like "I wrote all the music and Donna and Pete would add the lyrics" reflect a tendency to inflate his own role, and minimize those of the core "team" (Moroder, Bellotte, and Kueppers). In the same interview, he also contradicts himself by acknowledging that after returning from a European tour, Summer "listened to the tape of music I had arranged and wrote the entire album with Pete Bellotte in just a few days." Bellotte has roundly dismissed his version of events and restricts Esty's role to "arranger of the strings and brass, not a writer or producer," adding that "he was a transitory figure in our lives," not to mention "disliked by all the musicians."[10] What isn't disputed is the lightning speed at which Donna Summer recorded her vocals—just one day for each of the sides of an LP. According to Bellotte, she would generally arrive in at around three or four in the afternoon, strictly on her own schedule. After arriving she would "chat, chat and chat" then, suddenly realizing the time, would "go into the vocal booth, generally nail it in the first take" before

---

[10] Esty did supply some more specific detail about the arrangement process itself, that he "wrote out all the charts for the rhythm section" and also got paid a flat fee for doing a "synthesizer demo of the whole album," based on Moroder's original chords. He also credited Bellotte for coming in later for guitar overdubs.

disappearing again. No diva when it came to the precision of her recordings, Summer hated to "waste time" in the studio. Capturing the feeling of the moment was more important than laboring away on fussy would-be masterpieces. As with *Four Seasons of Love* and *I Remember Yesterday*, she was also heavily involved in writing the lyrics on this album together with Bellotte (a process, that according to Esty, happened after the rest of the recording had been completed). Just the background vocals then needed to be added as she continued her tour of Europe.[11]

The year 1977 proved to be typically busy for Moroder. Alongside the two Donna Summer projects that came out of Musicland, there was also his solo album *From Here to Eternity*, Roberta Kelly's *Zodiac Lady*, the debut LP from Munich Machine, and Dino Solera's mostly forgotten disco-crossover *Classically Dino Solera*. Act 2 of *Once Upon A Time* was essentially the next progression, along with *From Here to Eternity* in the pioneering sequencer sound developed in "I Feel Love" earlier in the year. The tracks on the Side 2 suite share the trancey qualities of "I Feel Love," thanks to their programmed close synchronization. While "I Feel Love" was

---

[11] There's a story that circulated very widely on the internet about Summer's health during the recording of *Once Upon A Time*. According to an (uncited) radio interview, Summer stated that she was hospitalized for exhaustion after recording for three days straight. Moroder has been asked specifically about the truth of this and has denied it. No mention is made in her autobiography of a hospitalization after these sessions either. This may just be a case of wires getting crossed about timings—certainly the worst of her battles with mood and exhaustion seemed to be under control by the end of 1977.

staged from relatively simple elements (according to Bellotte no more than two or three at the same time), the Side 2 tracks are far more complex, layered with "all sorts of ethereal things" in the background. Unlike the melding of man and machine explored in Kraftwerk's robot pop, which verges on the utopian, these three songs don't feel so much like a celebration of technology. "Working The Midnight Shift," the centerpiece of Act 2, contains more of an implied critique. The most immediately striking thing about the track, with its long instrumental introduction, is the atmosphere—a harsh strip-lit blues immediately invoked within the icy descending arpeggios. Just a few years away, the work anthems of the 1980s—Dolly Parton's "9 to 5" or Huey Lewis' "Workin' for a Livin'," for example—became irresistibly peppy, their grousing still upbeat and good-natured. "Working the Midnight Shift," however, shares none of this optimism; this is work made audibly dystopian. A lot of this happens in the rhythmic aspects of the track. Busy arpeggios regulate the pulse throughout, suggesting hands in constant, relentless motion. The piston introduced in "Now I Need You" comes and goes here, as if phasing in and out of the worker's consciousness. The most disturbing aspect of the song comes from the singer, who sounds barely present in her situation, even as she blankly considers it. Earlier on Side 1, the breathy soprano in "Fairy Tale High" suggested a child lost in her fantasy, but the same voice here is emanating from an adult, trapped in exploitative labor even as she's "dying inside." The expression of disconnect from the body is almost complete, a chilling loss of corporeal agency. As if in some Fordist nightmare, it seems that she's forgotten how to stop, an automaton carrying out functions according to her programming. If the disembodied voice feels somehow familiar, that's because it's essentially the same one used in "I Feel Love." But there's a big difference in the context between the two. The transcendent glory of "I Feel Love" comes from how it projects astrally up into the ecstatic galaxies of love(making); an out-of-body experience also appears to happen in "Working The Midnight Shift," but this time it's triggered by fatigue and the banality of routine.

As for what the job actually entails, well, that's never really clarified. The effect on the listener is that they are free to insert their own experiences of late-night work into the scenario, whether as taxi drivers, bartenders, sweatshop seamstresses, or security guards. As with most lyrics, the reluctance to pin down specifics makes it all the more universal. Someone I know imagined on hearing the album that the singer was a bartender in a sex club —it's probably no coincidence that this is one of the jobs he does himself. However, the most common interpretation, given both the time setting (and Summer's later indelible image in "She Works Hard for the Money") is that the singer is a waitress in a late-night diner. Whatever the work is, the music lasers in on the menial aspects of tasks involved. It's predictable that the song rests largely in a melancholic minor key. However, the chorus plays against type by switching from minor to major, providing an unexpected burst of sweetness. It may be sweet, but it's also somehow creepy, like Christina Ricci trying to force a smile in *Addams Family Values*. If Act 1 is defined by melodrama, Act 2 changes gear to mild horror.

There's another marginal interpretation of the song worth exploring—the possibility that the singer is, in fact, a sex worker, and the "Midnight Shift" her beat. If this theme comes easily to mind within Donna Summer's music, it's really her own fault—she had a habit of singing about fallen women throughout the 1970s and on her most famous album cover, *Bad Girls,* poses in full street walker attire. "Bad Girls," the song, was just the latest in a series of such portraits; early singles like "Virgin Mary" and "Lady of the Night" acted as practice runs, the latter matter-of-factly depicting sex work *as* work with the empathetic observation "it's just a job but she'll do the best she can." Erasure's Andy Bell also subscribes to the Cinderella-as-sex worker theory, and in his imagination, "the café was a guise—probably she was working the streets outside." The colorful career path he imagined for Cinderella from hooker (or rather *super* hooker in her "Charlie's Angels tights and Olivia Newton John tops") to princess may at first sound like a cultural outlier. But it's not. Often thought of as one of the earliest Cinderella tales, in the Greek story of Rhodopsis, the title character is a courtesan slave girl who marries the king of Egypt. If we then shift our focus to cinema (most obviously Julia Roberts' character Vivian Ward in *Pretty Woman*), a pattern emerges that make such interpretations look fairly well grounded. Sex-working Cinderellas are a common trope in cinema, from *Pretty Woman* to Audrey Hepburn's high-class whore in *Breakfast at Tiffanys* (with Truman Capote as fairy godfather). The pattern is a global one too. *Lọ Lem Hè Phố,* a 2004 Vietnamese comedy/drama, has the English title of "Street Cinderella" and 2007's *Year of the Fish* adapts "Ye Xian," the best-known Chinese Cinderella.

Like *Once Upon A Time, Year of the Fish* has a New York setting, but this version has sees Cinderella's late mother's cousin unsuccessfully trying to coerce her into sex work in a massage parlor.

The fantasy in *Pretty Woman* isn't just romantic, it's also consumerist. Let loose in a strip of high-end fashion boutiques with a borrowed credit card, Vivian shops till she drops in what is, for the audience, an intoxicating *Supermarket Sweep* of consumerist desire. It's essentially an inversion of the fairy godmother transformation scene, with Richard Gere's businessman, Edward Lewis, playing Pygmalion/fairy godfather behind the scenes. We're encouraged to root for the underdog, as Vivian puts the snooty attendants in their place, but the shopping scenes have drawn the criticism of feminists for their sexist dynamics (men produce/women consume). This aspect of *Pretty Woman* is quintessential Cinderella, whose story has become intimately bound up with fashion. Clothes, as most of us instinctively realize, are an effective way to deceive the eye and ascend the social ladder. In Perrault's version of the tale, one of two final morals is that "it's kindness more than dress, that can win a man's heart, with greater success." There might be some fundamental misreading of human nature going on here, as more and more sociological studies seem to confirm the old maxim of "what is beautiful is good"—that human beings make a connection between physical beauty and positive traits.

At the turn of the twentieth century, fashion became a democratizing power as department stores started opening up everywhere. Perrault may not have been able to predict it, but writers of the time certainly noticed. Cinderella musicals quickly sprang up like the 1905 operetta *Mlle. Modiste*, or *Irene* in 1919. Both of them centered on aspiring shop-girl-Cinderellas, whose access to clothes allowed them to dupe high society into thinking they were one of them. Shop girls were cheap sources of labor working long shop hours, so the possibilities of social mobility through fashion became a compelling narrative device. Seen in this particular light, the reasons why the Summer Cinderella compromises herself to work the midnight shift become transparent as a glass slipper—she understands the power of changing her appearance. Shoes made of glass, ribbons, lace—the visual language is the same as the Disney/Perrault tale, but how Cinderella manages to acquire them are something quite different. The transformation of the exterior, particularly for women, became increasingly important as the decades of the twentieth century rolled by, and it began to be seen as part of the "cure" for a number of ills. By the 1950s, beauty had become firmly aligned with therapy and it was in this decade that the makeover show *Queen for a Day* debuted on American television. Subtitled as the "Cinderella Show," *Queen for a Day* ran five days a week from 1956–1964. Every episode saw dowdy contestants in downtrodden situations competing for audience sympathy that, if successful, would grant them a show coronation. There had to be a sob story (polio-stricken children pretty much sums up the tone) and a suitably modest wish to move the audience's emotions (perhaps a gurney *for* the polio-stricken child?). Of course, the gurney was never the real prize. Instead, the winner was showered with a cornucopia of consumer goods provided by the sponsors. Washing machines, floor waxers—they weren't always what the queen needed, but perhaps neither was the makeover and new wardrobe of designer dresses. After all, when the ball came to a close, the queen-for-a-day would have to return to the patriarchal culture that created and constrained her. The fantasy was nonetheless intoxicating for 1950s housewives, keeping the audience in a consumerist trance, even as critics condemned them as exploitative "misery shows."

In conventional Cinderella stories, for this transformation to be able to happen, a fairy godmother must sparkle into life to save the day, often prompted by the wretched tears of the heroine (catnip for susceptible godmothers apparently). The arrival of the godmother is also usually the cue for an upbeat song. The transformation song is often a high point in musical adaptations, certainly the jolliest. "Bibbidi Bobbidi Boo" in the Disney version and "It's Impossible" in Rodgers and Hammerstein's are both easily the most memorable in each film, as they rapidly turn around Cinderella's fortunes. More recently, though, there has been a trend of simply dispensing with the fairy godmother entirely. If there is some kind of a replacement, this is often now personal attributes like "feistiness." It's understandable why. As part of a re-evaluation of what girls actually *need* from fairytales, a Deusa Ex Machina solving problems with a flick of the wand isn't necessarily the thing. The modern answer to how Cinderella moves beyond her circumstances involves some form of self-reliance, and so it is in *Once Upon A Time*.

Side 2's "Queen for a Day" is also a hypnotic waking dream—of a girl sat at the dressing table, considering her transformation in the mirror. It catches her at the point of preparing to go out dancing, in an imaginative trance of being the belle of the ball. At points like these, it's easy to see how Donna Summer had her young daughter Mimi in mind while writing the songs. The fantasies she returns to are often childish ones, which rub shoulders alongside much more adult content. The subject matter and mood is a big change from the previous song, but the genius of Act 2's music really is in the detail. Subtle continuity runs across the three tracks as the atmosphere phases like a mood lamp. In the last two of these tracks, the harsh blue of the "Midnight Shift" gives way to a warm and glowing pink and, as this happens, a lot of the sound detail from one flows into another. The constant agitation of "Midnight Shift's" arpeggiated bass line in "Queen for a Day" doesn't disappear but evolves into the light clatter of a flanging sixteenth beat, and work transitions seamlessly into leisure. The suggestion of the music (anticipating modern anxieties about the work/leisure divide) is that the two are intimately connected. As a perfumed cloud of prettification whirls around the singer, the restless hands that were previously in service of labor now apply themselves to the details of glamor. Within her fuzzy solipsism, something is also conjured of the comforting glow of Christmas—a busier version of Paul McCartney's "Wonderful Christmastime" perhaps. Spun-sugar electrosonics glisten around the voice, and bulbous broken synthesizer chords hang decoratively like the frosted baubles on a Christmas tree.

Then, two-thirds of the way into the track, in one of the most inspired production choices on the album, the music abruptly switches from a purely electronic production to a full live band with strings. It's a startling moment that, on first exposure, caused Jimmy Somerville to think he was going to "piss myself." It also marks a dividing point in the album, laying down the boundary between the two main dimensions (fantasy and real) of the story, the moment where Cinderella steps out into the real world, which here means the disco. Not *everybody* got it, though. Davitt Sigerson's piece on disco in the *Sounds* column "New Musick" remarked that "because the arrangement is identical, it takes a few moments to notice just what has happened. Nothing has happened, except that Moroder switches from synthesising Moogs to synthesising musicians." Perhaps some people were more attuned than others. In the move from private to public, a kind of coming out of the closet occurs, just one way that the shift is loaded with queer metaphorical potential. In another analogy, it's an equivalent in sound of the famous transition from black and white to color in *The Wizard of Oz*. In Edward Buscombe's 1978 essay on film sound and color, he argues that the switch in the 1939 film wasn't just an advert for the new Technicolor film process, but a self-reflexive celebration of technology in film itself. It was as if the moment was saying "look how marvelous the cinema is." "Queen for a Day" works along the same lines, except it's travelling in the other direction. We don't step into the magical world of technological music but out of it and the message is the opposite of Oz—"see how wonderful real, organic life is." On the other side of the boundary, there's an expansive new prairie of sound waiting with its ringing piano and cheerful string comps. It manages to be less cluttered than the electrodisco Christmas that precedes it, but in its own way is just as exuberant. There's joy in both halves, evenly matched perhaps, but the sound of the live sequence is a far worldlier kind of joy. Finally, the singer has taken her head out of the clouds and planted her two feet on the ground. She is now dancing rather than just dreaming about dancing.

The close of Act 2 ultimately feels like a kind of liberation, a giant step into the unknown. Mikal Gilmore had his own interpretation—Acts 1 and 2 were the unfolding of "Cinderella's dream—to be free of the machines." The symbolic moment at the end of "Queen for a Day" is a beacon, offering hope that she has indeed achieved her dream, and escaped from the machine's heartless grasp. Yet, when he reviewed Donna Summer's self-titled album in 1982, after five short years, the NME's Barney Hoskyns was already in nostalgia mode. He lamented the disappearance of "the lost disco goddess of *Once Upon A Time*" and found himself still swimming in "the rapturous ethereal straits of 'Now I Need You' or 'Working The Midnight Shift.'" Some of us are swimming there still. Maybe there's magic in the machine after all.

# Brief Interlude
# A Man Like You or How to
# Get Your Man

So, Cinderella. You wake up one day and you know that it's time—time to go get yourself that man. You're primped, puffed and perfumed to perfection, and your destiny awaits you in the disco. But what happens now? How exactly *do* you bag a prince? The answer is in Act 3 and the process turns out to be messier than a night on the tiles with Courtney Love. When a classic Cinderella enters the ballroom, she is prized for her serenity. Like a swan, she is expected to glide weightlessly across the marble floor, to be claimed by the prince who immediately recognizes her grace and glowing beauty. But not this one. She's only going to bag the prize with literal sweat and tears that will be wrung out with a great deal of effort on the dancefloor. As a consequence, Act 3 ends up being earthier, and a whole lot earthlier, than the rest of the album—the odd one out of the four acts in several ways. It's not only Cinderella who gets freed from the machine after Act 2. For a few songs at least, the music goes lateral, exploring a variety of styles without the metric restraints imposed on the other sides. It feels more human too, probably because we get the only tangible representations of other human beings in the story (nasty though they may be). Finally, it's a side of action as, out in the real world, Cinderella tries her best to make things *happen.*

It makes more sense in some ways to think of *Once Upon A Time* as having a two-act rather than the four-act structure that was mostly imposed by the time limitations of vinyl pressing. This way, it's much easier to compare the album to a Broadway musical, the format that was clearly in the back of its producers' minds as they made the record. Classic two-act musical structure generally leaves the audience at the intermission with, if not a cliffhanger, then at least a question in their minds, something that makes them want to come back and see it resolved. "How will she fare out in the real world?" is probably the best we have here, but it kind of works. After the introspective electro-blues on the previous side, the beginning of Act 3 is a rapid turnaround, but the contrast in scenario between the two pairs of acts is also classic Broadway. It's a Cinderella radically transformed that we meet as it opens, newly confident and assertive. It's clear that the process of beautifying her exterior in "Queen for a Day" has been a *success*, and with the battle armor to go forth into the disco and conquer, that's exactly what she does (if only she described what she was actually wearing).

The song that introduces this new persona, "If You Got It, Flaunt It," is so immediate, that any memory of the midnight shift is swept away. A brassy disco cakewalk with military style drums and classic walking bassline, it throws us right into the heart of the action. Up until now, the female vocalists in the choir have been used exclusively to support the main singer. Here, they emerge from the chorus and briefly assume a role of their own, becoming a phalanx of catty party goers. As the competition for Cinderella, they're the closest we get to ugly sisters in the story, and "Flaunt It" is effectively their theme song, even if they only get to do the backing vocals. Like an evil twist on the *Soul Train* line dance, the ladies swipe viciously at their new rival as she bravely struts her way down the gauntlet of the dancefloor. The expression "if you've got it, flaunt it" seems to have been around forever but, in fact, cropped up first in a scene from the 1967 Mel Brooks film *The Producer*. It was only popularized shortly afterwards in the late 1960s after Braniff Airlines used it in their "Plane Plain" campaign. "Flaunt" is an odd choice of word to use in a song, especially when it's repeated eighteen times (try saying it out loud over and over again). But the song is effective enough, borrowing its attitude and blues-based chord patterns from Labelle's 1974 hit "Lady Marmalade" and its famous cheerleading intro "hey sister, go sister, soul sister." "If You Got It Flaunt It" effectively reverses the mantra, which now becomes the put-down "sister thinks she's got it," chased along by a sassy finger-wagging tag of "who do you think you are." Patti Labelle may have claimed innocence of the fact (incredibly), but Bob Crewe's lyrics for "Lady Marmalade" were inspired by the street walkers he saw while walking around New Orleans. Despite the similarities in musical and lyrical tone, Summer's Cinderella, even if we were to subscribe to the sex worker reading, is no Lady Marmalade. The cutthroat swagger she has suddenly acquired is an eye-opening development after the introversion established for her character in the previous sides. Her new attitude isn't completely owned, though, just borrowed long enough so that she can hold her space for the duration of the song. What's also really noticeable, when looking back from this track to "Working the Midnight Shift," is how dramatically the singer's relationship with her body has shifted. From a complete dissolution of bodily agency earlier, she now has a formidable mastery over it. "I can shake my hip, or my thigh," she boasts, seemingly with a puppeteer's control over every last sinew. It's an even more remarkable turnaround from Act 1, where we witnessed the same character practically running from her shadow in "Faster and Faster to Nowhere." Now, with her body weaponized and on the attack, it's not Cinderella on the run, but her competition. In no other Cinderella story is dance itself presented as such a battle, not even in the vigorous jiving in *Cindy*.

Once again, *Once Upon A Time* deviated from Summer's life story, and the combative nightlife scenarios of Act 3 were very different from how she went about initiating her own relationships. These often developed quite spontaneously out of encounters in the entertainment world in which she worked, meeting many of her boyfriends in bands and theatre shows. It was while recording *I Remember Yesterday* in 1977 that she would first encounter the man who would become her second husband, and partner until her death— Bruce Sudano. Their first meeting occurred when he was providing backing vocals on her album with his soulful disco group Brooklyn Dreams, although it didn't take place in the studio, but in the house of a mutual friend –Summer's manager Susan Munao. For a woman whose public image was larger than life, involving some impressive wigs, after meeting Sudano her game plan to bag the man she wanted to marry was directed the other way, by ditching the glamor. Off came the wigs, and Sudano's eligibility was tested with a display of her natural hair. "Either you like it or you don't," she said, pointing at her head. As history proved, it was a highly successful way of coming out of the hair closet.

Although the Act is organized around a consistent theme—trying to get the man—and is nominally set in and around the disco, the sequence of events through which this happens is wonderfully chaotic. Across the four songs (and a brief instrumental reprise of the title track), the singer attempts to lure the man, then loses him, cries a lot, and throws herself back on the dancefloor (unsuccessfully it seems) to try and get him again. She's a hot mess in more ways than one. Much of this happens within the disco, but some of it confusingly appears not to. "Sweet Romance," which is placed in the middle of the suite, has a line "I can't sleep from crying" that suggests she went home and came back again another night. As Cinderella stories go, it's all getting rather confusing, although at this point, it's probably not worth losing your own sleep worrying over the details. When the curtain rises on Act 3, it's the first time the music and the narrative setting completely fuse together. We hear disco music, as in the rest of the album, but until now we haven't had lyrics that also take place *within* a disco. The medium has finally become the story. This was no innovation on the part of Summer, Bellotte, and Moroder. By the end of 1977, songs that dealt in romance and/or dancing in the disco (Joe Tex' "Ain't Gonna Bump No More," for example) were established practice. Many of the songs name-checked the genre in their titles too, like "Disco

Inferno" and "Disco Duck." More than any genre of dance music in its history to date, disco constantly references its locale within its lyrics, a reflection, perhaps, of the rapid commercial processes that turned the disco experience out as a tight-packaged commodity. Already in 1976, The Ritchie Family's hit "The Best Disco in Town" took the idea to its extreme by cramming in an orgy of disco quotations (including "Love to Love You Baby"). More than a disco story, it functioned as advertisement too, with the Ritchie girls hard-selling the disco experience by parading some of its greatest hits. *Once Upon A Time*'s own meta-commentary on disco didn't go unnoticed in Stephen Holden's incisive review for *Rolling Stone*. The one piece that really wanted to peek behind the sequin curtain for deeper meanings came from a rock critic—perhaps no surprise—but that Holden took a disco album as seriously as he did is remarkable in itself. "Could *Once Upon A Time* be a critique of the voluptuary subculture that is sure to devour it like candy?" he mused, before answering his own question in typically florid style:

> Moroder and Bellotte's aural style equates glamor and shallowness with such a glacial detachment that it seems sadistic. The music reflects the tawdry orgy palace atmosphere—Versailles for the masses—that stands for elegance in the disco business, and then refrains from animating that atmosphere with a single drop of warmth; instead it pricks and mocks.

Out of context, the quote sounds like it's expressing revulsion for the album, but Holden, in his own way, was expressing admiration for how it seemed to prod interrogatively at its own genre. It's just one example of where critics, including myself, keep finding angles in the subject matter that were probably very distant from its creators' minds. Years later, Summer claimed her personal inspiration for making the album was "just a little fairy tale album" that she wrote "for my daughter." Moroder himself dismissed interpretations of his music as "art," preferring to think of it unpretentiously as just pop music. There's an irony in the choice of styles across Act 3, though. Although bookended with two tracks set in the disco ("Dance into my Life" and the opener "If You Got It Flaunt It"), it doesn't actually double down on typical disco material. Instead, the suite houses more traditional ballads and all the songs can be said to use less standard disco tempos. This created a variety of pace and diversity of style that many critics appreciated. DJs, however, generally gave the side a wide berth, only coaxing play out of "If You Got It Flaunt It." Without it, the album may have been in danger of wearing out its audience with an overlong high-tempo marathon. It's a surprising choice for the one act where we might *expect* disco music to dominate, but by subverting the expectation, Side 3 manages to neatly sidestep the corniness of "The Best Disco in Town."

Bellotte felt that Act 3 was an opportunity for Summer to let loose and showcase more of her gospel roots—an "Aretha, Etta James kind of feel" as he put it. Performing the ballad "A Man Like You" in a 1978 episode of *The Midnight Special*, she channels Bessie Smith, perching (somewhat stiffly) on the edge of the stage in a voluminous ostrich-feather coat. For a change, the singer puts aside the "obsessive interior monologue" that Holden's review noticed and delivers the song straight-up/no-frills as a conventional R&B ballad. And for the first time on *Once Upon A Time*, when she sings about a man, it sounds as if she's addressing a flesh-and-blood person, rather than a storybook fantasy. It's tempting to imagine she was thinking of Sudano.

"A Man Like You" was recognized by many as a strong album cut, but unlike some of her 1970s contemporaries—Roberta Flack or early solo-career Diana Ross for example—the public was reluctant to embrace Donna Summer for her ballads. A supremely versatile vocalist, it was far from the case that she couldn't sing them, but the particular route her success took meant that ballads ended up being pursued more as a sideline. It could perhaps have been otherwise. *Four Seasons of Love's* gentle country ballad "Winter Melody" was a modest chart success and must have encouraged Casablanca to push another ballad as lead single from her next album. When radio passed on "Can't We Just Sit Down and Talk It Over" and picked up on its B-Side "I Feel Love," the sides were famously flipped. From then on, few ballads were tried out as singles and only the steamy "Woman in Me" had any noticeable chart success (33 on the Hot 100 in 1982). Inspirational sign-offs like "I Believe In Jesus" or "Let There Be Peace" got tucked away at the back of albums, making them easier to ignore if you didn't appreciate the message or style. It was in live work where Summer could fully inhabit her favorite MOR songs (Streisand's "The Way We Were"), bluesy standards ("The Man I Love"), or the gospel interludes she introduced into her shows in the 1980s.

"A Man Like You" is delivered back-to-back with another ballad, but the second one has a very different feel. Holden's review noted the high camp in "Sweet Romance," summing it up as "hilariously praying to 'father dear' with a quasi-baroque harpsichord behind her." Beloved of the French orchestra leader Paul Mauriat, by the mid-1970s, the harpsichord was at the kitschy tail end of a long fashion wave. More often than not, it would now end up smooshed together with syrupy violins in something approaching the breathy soft porn of the *Emmanuele* soundtracks. The harpsichord (or more accurately electro-spinet in its synthetic version) also briefly found its way into disco, via faux-Spanish–French disco act Bimbo Jet and their hit "El Bimbo." Its use in "Sweet Romance" has more of the hushed acoustic environment of the confessional chamber, threading through the music in an elegant, if slightly cheesy, counterpoint to Summer's melody. Just as with "Now I Need You," "father dear" is ambiguous but here less so, tilting towards the church and fitting in a song tradition that would later take in Madonna songs like "Papa Don't Preach" and "Oh Father."

The way her autobiography tells it, most of the men in her life prior to Sudano, if not father figures *per se*, were in some way controlling, if not downright domineering. This was despite Summer having a feisty side herself. Hoby, an early boyfriend from her first band Crow, enjoyed playing Pygmalion to her unschooled Eliza Doolittle. And while she respected Neil Bogart, he, too, had a tendency to overplay the Svengali figure. The eagerness to grow and learn seemed to draw her to men that had something to teach, but this would often create power imbalances that could prove traumatic to equilibrate. When Gunther, the last boyfriend she had before Sudano, was deported back to Germany after subjecting her to a final, gun-assisted fit of jealous rage, she recalled being "finally free, yet terrified to be alone." During post-partum depression after Mimi's birth, she also recounted a visit from a former affair from the Munich years—a Dr. Meyer. When he discovered how she'd let herself fall into such a conventional domestic life, he chided her that "he'd always known I would sacrifice my career and settle for second best." Given her precarious mental state at the time, the comments were devastating. But change was around the corner, and magical destiny called once more. Within months, she had left the marriage and met Moroder, the man who would become her musical partner.

As a parting thought for this interlude, it's worth considering in all this what Donna Summer's *real* magical destiny was. True love, which, after several false starts, she eventually found in Bruce Sudano? Or was it the fulfilment of her artistic ambitions, the dream of childhood, which had been guilty of sidelining partners in her earlier relationships? If *Once Upon A Time* was her "life story in reality," was the fairy tale the success that her career had brought her? It seemed that, in Sudano, the man with whom she recorded, toured, and shared the parenting of three children, she ultimately got both.

# 4
# Fairy Tale High: A Personal Reading of *Once Upon A Time*

*Once Upon A Time (the late 1980s to be precise), a boy lived in a quiet and well-to-do village, just outside the road that encircles London. The city was far away, but not so far that it wasn't familiar from occasional visits. Like many queer teenagers at that time, the boy wasn't ready to reveal himself to the world. And so, in secret, he put himself together piece-by-piece. Dreaming a new persona into existence, he used whatever cultural bric-a-brac was lying around. One day he came across a disco record in the village shop. It looked worn and unloved, but on the front was a beautiful woman. When he opened the sleeve, she appeared again, towering like a giantess over the bright lights of a city. Was she a princess, a goddess, or an angel? There was only one way to find out. In those days, people laughed if you listened to disco—only queers liked that. So the boy laughed to himself, and couldn't think of a better reason to buy it. However, as he became an adolescent, the boy's confusion about life had forced him deep inside himself. Drifting out of sociality into awkwardness, he became ever more remote from friends and family. Around his fragile* mind, a thick forest of protecting thorns grew, and there inside the boy lived alone with his fantasies. In his little village, he was nowhere. One day, though, he knew he would escape to the metropolis and be famous like the girl on the record. There he would go to clubs and discos and make his mark (even though he had never so much as set foot in a disco before). The queer folk of the city would welcome him with open and understanding arms. Until then he would wait patiently, safe in the knowledge that in the land of dreams unreal, nothing could touch him.

When his day finally came to arrive in the city, nothing was quite as he imagined, and nobody was waiting at the gates of queer disco utopia to welcome him. In fact, it didn't really seem like utopia at all. Instead of dancing as he had in front of his mirror at home, he froze in the company of indifferent eyes. Many nights he would cry on the way home. The problem, he eventually realised, lay within himself. His fantasy of himself in the city was an evil lie of his own making, a deep hole from which he was struggling to climb out. Listening to the record again, suddenly he understood the princess in a new light. She was just like him—a sad dreamer with a too-fertile imagination. Perhaps, to keep her fragile mind from shattering, she too had retreated into the comfort of her fantasy world. What if she never married her prince? Perhaps she had never even met him in the first place! Suddenly it all became clear—the end of her tale was a pretty but empty lie. Years later, all grown up and with the sadness of the past behind him, an opportunity came to write a book, and tell people how he saw the story. The disco isn't the place where dreams came true. Sometimes it's the opposite: a place where the mirrors on the wall show you nothing but your failings.

This is the story of how I arrived at my reading of the album. Time has shown me that it's undeniably one shaped by my own queer subjectivity. I may have tidied up some of the details—stories, after all, are just stories—but the basic elements are all fundamentally true. My way of looking at things is highly personal, of course, shaped by the events in my own life. You will undoubtedly have your own way. But the idea in this chapter is to sift forensically through some of the clues that led *me* here, in the hope that it will perhaps bring *us* that bit closer to the album and some of the rich subtexts that swirl within it. I may be guilty of over-reaching with my conclusions and insights, but I make no apologies for this. It's in the interpretation that something becomes truly yours, and through the process or thinking and writing about *Once Upon A Time*, I've made it my own. Queer readings of *Once Upon a Time* are not just possible, but likely, given the fact that Donna Summer is by far the most-favored disco singer among gay men. This is just one of them.

Disco, as Tom Smucker recognized in his 1979 *The Village Voice* piece, became the first pop music with an openly gay component, and this section of the audience was instrumental in helping propel acts towards mainstream success, as happened with Donna Summer. Even allegations that she had decreed AIDS as God's punishment couldn't sever her bond with the gay audience, although it certainly tested it for a while. There's a twist in the timing, though. In his *Guardian* obituary, Paul Flynn saw her as the last gay icon to emerge who *didn't* pander to her gay audience, as Diana Ross did in her Chic-produced period. However, as Summer's career progressed, she soon became well aware of their existence and professed to having many gay friends and acquaintances. Many of Donna Summer's songs became gay anthems, despite being produced "under the tutorship of a hot-blooded heterosexual producer and his faithfully married lyricist in a sterile Munich hit factory" (as Flynn reads it). Part of her records' gay appeal was in their subject matter, and a lot of this, inevitably, came down to sex. The unashamed carnality of "Love to Love You Baby" clearly hit the spot, and there are plenty of other numbers that chime, whether intentionally or not, with gay sexual lifestyles. The wide-eyed sex-venturer in *Bad Girls'* "Lucky," for example, delivers a splendidly breezy ode to the casual encounter, anticipating George Michael's "Fast Love" decades later. Another part of her appeal was the visual image that delved into the high fantasy of science fiction and Egyptiana. She could also be extremely camp in performance, delighting in play acting innocence and fluttering her eyelashes, even as what she sang pushed beyond innuendo into full-blown sexual expression.

*Once Upon A Time* seems to have a special place in gay men's hearts. In *Out* Magazine's "Greatest, Gayest Albums (of all time)," it landed at No. 72 (although the bigger-selling *Bad Girls* ranked higher at 34 and *Living Proof*, a live album by Sylvester, the *other* queen of disco, even higher at 24). The strongest advocates of the album are often gay men, and high-profile ones at that. Jimmy Somerville, whose group Bronski Beat had a European hit with a medley that included "I Feel Love" and "Love to Love You Baby," considers it "possibly one of the best concept albums ever" and Erasure's Andy Bell also put it on his thirteen favorite albums list in *The Quietus*. Bell later reminisced to me about how, many years after its release in the mid-1980s, it formed part of the soundtrack to the flamboyant atmosphere in one of the last gay co-operative houses in London. With its subtexts of escapism, loneliness, and nightlife transformation, there's plenty to speak to queer sensibilities.

"Love to Love You Baby" wasn't made with a gay audience in mind, but often it seems like some of her subsequent repertoire is just too knowing for its queer appeal simply to be a coincidence. As any keyed-in listener would have known—and queer men were fully in the program—the kinds of high that you were likely find in a disco were generally chemical ones; in disco's earlier years, acid and quaaludes dominated the intake, in its latter ones, coke. Unlike more counter-cultural movements—psychedelia and confessional rock or, later on, hip-hop and acid house—disco played it coy when it came to making direct references to drugs. Mention of them is generally avoided in its lyrics and naming a disco song "Fairy Tale High" was in itself exceptional for the genre. Even then, the song is only guilty of winking at its audience as an adult joke, daring them to take its title at face value. Inside, it's stuffed like a piñata with sugary drug allusions and you may well find yourself wondering just what is causing the eyes to "brighten." The delicious fun lies in how these allusions are set off against a pre-teen sleepover atmosphere that's not a million miles away from the innocent crush of "Love's Unkind." A lot of this is captured in the deliberately naïve melody, which has the comforting rise-and-fall symmetry of a lullaby or nursery rhyme. The chorus takes the melodic scheme even further, descending a full major octave step-wise, like a learner practicing their first book of piano scales.[1] Even more immediately, there's the cutie-pie delivery of Summer's vocals, which are laid on double-thick to drive the double-meaning home. Ironically, given its title, the track studiously avoids the musical methods tested out in the disco-lab of *actually* getting dancers high—fast tempos, pulsing basslines, pounding drums and anthemic choruses. Compare "Fairy Tale High" with "Hi Energy," Evelyn Thomas' crackling theme tune for the electronic successor to disco, where the same formula was perfected. In the most startling moment in the song, Thomas launches like a rocket up into the stratosphere on the word "high," with the music and lyric in full complement. An even better word than stratosphere for this airless zone is the *poppersphere*, given gay men's topical use of the inhalant during rush moments in their favorite songs. The "high" of "Fairy Tale High," despite the drug allusions and sparkling disco synthsonics, is distinctly lacking in whoooosh, trading instead in cutesy double handclaps. The textures in the chorus give a little more away with a star sprinkle of sugary synths, whose connection with cocaine would be finally sealed in Melle Mel's "White Lines" five years later. There is also a point later in the instrumental breakdown/build-up where there *could* be a drug scenario taking place—a backing chant repeating "on a fairy tale high ... getting *higher and higher*." As the chant builds, handclaps now hit on every

---

[1] This melody was, in fact, recycled from another Moroder/Bellotte project from the same year—Moroder's solo album *From Here to Eternity*, released only three months prior to *Once Upon A Time*. The title track, a wide-eyed love song which became a hit across Europe, was Moroder's only solo UK top 20 chart single.

beat of the bar, together with a low, pounding tom-tom. You can almost imagine her surrounded by a chorus of drug enablers, or the tripped-out members of a cult, goading her on. Out of the context of the album, the number is perhaps a little too saccharine for its own good. Released as a single in South Africa and Germany, as with the title track it had little chart success. Within the sequencing of Act 2, though, there's something intriguingly off about the sweetness, sandwiched as it is between two far more aggressive numbers, "Faster and Faster to Nowhere" and "Say Something Nice." It's the sequencing that allows you to look at the song in a different light, indicating for the first time that her state of mind can turn on a dime. In the depths of despair one minute, elated the next, the extreme oscillation of her mood raises some questions; if we can't explain this by clues from her external reality, the place we will inevitably look for them is her interior world. In songwriting, as often with life, psychological drama is generally the more rewarding place to dwell.

The song seems to be proof that the narrator is, if not necessarily unreliable, then certainly unstable. The character is not a million miles away from the clumsy singleton (with a serious case of arrested development) in the Australian comedy *Muriel's Wedding*, a film which is itself highly gay-coded. The overweight and socially awkward Muriel spends most of the film dreaming of her perfect fairy tale wedding, but when she finally achieves her dream (a sham wedding in a marriage of convenience) it happens via a toxic bouquet of self-deception. Muriel looks to a disco song to provide the ultimate yardstick of how fulfilled her life actually is—ABBA's "Dancing Queen." She knows that when her life in Sydney is as good as "Dancing Queen" she's made it, measuring her changing reality against the feeling she gets from the song. The brilliance of the film, and much of the comedy, derives from the tension between Muriel's obsessive fantasy about the perfect wedding, and the tragedies she is constantly trying to bury (her best friend's cancer diagnosis and paralysis, the implosion of her dysfunctional family). "Fairy Tale High" is fully conscious that life isn't a fairy tale, but, like *Muriel's Wedding*, it hinges on the same deception that life could be *like* a fairy tale if you only pretend hard enough; "I've told so many lies I don't even know I'm doing it" realizes Muriel towards the film's conclusion. Still, there is something provocative about using the word "high" in the context of a feminized childhood, where "fun" and "high-spirited" would be more appropriate. In her poorly received TV special broadcast from 1980, Summer sings a version of the song as a lullaby to her daughter Mimi, then only six years old. Mimi falls asleep and dreams that she is singing her own version of "Fairy Tale High," styled (in full make-up) in the image of her mother. The words feel odd coming out of the mouth of a child but, sung by an adult persona, the song points to a reluctance to completely enter adult life, inhabiting the eerie permanent adolescence of the so-called "Peter Pan syndrome." Often associated with gay men because of certain leisure and cultural activities (a fixation on teen pop, going to dance parties often well into their forties and fifties), the term is often used as a slight, or evidence of a more disturbing underlying condition (see Michael Jackson).

This arrested development somehow found its way into the few songs that wrote openly on the subject of gay lives before disco, although they were often written and sung by straight men. Charles Aznavour's 1972 chanson "Comme Ils Disent" ("As They Say") frankly recounts the desires and disappointments of a gay man with a double life—performing a drag striptease by night, he keeps house with his mother during the day. The object of his desire (in the French version at least) was a heterosexual man, the love tragically unrequited. As with cinema and television, songs that explored the gay condition in the 1960s and early 1970s often ended with their protagonists unhappy, frustrated in one-way desire, or even dead, in the case of Rod Stewart's "The Killing of Georgie." Queer critics have been keen to dismiss this pattern, arguing that representing same-sex desire as doomed or impossible is an ideological choice, rather than a reflection of reality. If the UK's decriminalizing Sexual Offences Act of 1967 and the Stonewall Riots in the US in 1969 started to bring gay relationships into the light as more progressive attitudes to sexuality developed, the culture at least began to shift. Disco acted as a potent catalyst for change, as well as producing the first truly out-and-proud anthem, Valentino's "I Was Born This Way" in 1975. It fostered autonomous, sacred, and very sweaty spaces without the threat of raids and arrest where, for the first time, gay men could be sexually bold and experiment with new masculine identities. "What Makes A Man A Man" asked Aznavour in the English translation of "Comme Ils Disent"; by the end of the decade, thanks to the clone culture which emerged from the gay disco scene, you could perhaps be forgiven for thinking the answer was The Village People.

Although it's an emancipatory experience for many, for the shy, going to gay clubs can also be very intimidating, the first visits a trial by fire. When he began going to Heaven (London's biggest gay club at the time) every week during the early 1980s, Andy Bell was one of the shy ones. Painfully aware that for the macho clone crowd he was a "little queeny boy," he expected to be ignored and spent the first year standing by the wall, watching the crowd. He recalls the disco being a very lonely place, where the percentage of times you actually met somebody "was probably 5%." Often, the night would end up with him going home alone on the night bus, a kind of ritual purgatory for late-night Londoners that can amplify any underlying loneliness. The despondent trips home might have been among "the worst times ever" but he felt they also fed his inner strength, as if some kind of test of character and endurance. Act 3's finale, "Dance into my Life," hinges on this trial, and the fear of going home alone and unloved drives the urgency and drama of the song. As with "If You Got It, Flaunt It," the entire number takes place on the dancefloor, but is haunted by the same questions that have plagued Bell, myself and countless others looking for love. "What if I don't manage to connect with another person? How will I feel about myself at the end of the night if I go home alone?" The scenario may be a common one for many people, but in pop lyrics, the theme is mostly atypical. Songs about being a shy wallflower or crying your way home on the bus are, perhaps understandably, vastly outnumbered by those about having a good time. Yet sadness still has a place in dance music in the growing canon of what has come to be known as the "sad banger"—essentially upbeat dance tunes that are also laced with a beguiling melancholy (Ultra Naté's "Free," for example). In certain moods, tunes like Kool and the Gang's "Celebration" can feel oppressive to some of us, enforcing fun where it's really not welcome. It's also no surprise that ABBA's "Dancing Queen"—the totemic song of *Muriel's Wedding*—has been probed for its own melancholic subtexts: Angus Harrison's great article on the song in *Vice* Magazine interprets it as "a song about death," where the narrator is an older woman watching her youth slip away as she observes the younger one dancing. When the theme is expertly written, as with Robyn's modern classic "Dancing on my Own," the music can be truly incandescent, burning a hole directly through the senses into the heart. The trope, best summed up as "tears on the dance floor"[2] has history, going back at least as far as Lesley Gore's 1963 hit "It's My Party" (and I'll cry if I want to). It went on to maintain a foothold in the disco era—the "dance-to-keep-from-crying" theme of Carrie Lucas' "I Gotta Keep Dancin'" and later on, house music got its own sad disco anthem in Lil Louis' "Club Lonely." The best of these songs use dance music as a strategic tool, realizing that the beats that underpin them don't just reflect the setting, they *are* the setting. The story in "Dancing on My Own" of watching your old lover kiss his new one from the shadowy parts of the club is so heart-wrenching precisely because it's not a ballad. The introspection of the lyrics gets juxtaposed against the relentless thump of the beats and physicality of dancing—but that's why the pathos hits home. Such songs transmit in real time exactly what the moment feels like.

[2]Realizing the potential for mining the trope, British pop group Steps actually named their 2017 comeback album *Tears on the Dancefloor*.

If the disco is an unwelcoming place in "If You Got It, Flaunt It," this is doubly so in "Dance into my Life." Of all the sonic environments in which *Once Upon A Time* places its heroine, the song's verse is the most hostile—a rasping, desert soundscape, mixed to the consistency of baked parchment; shakers and guiros rustle menacingly from the borders, along with a rattlesnake vocoder wah. The title[3] suggests a straight disco stomper and the frenetic chorus, bumped along by bursts of timbales, almost makes it so. But there's a perverse fragmentation to the overall construction of the track that makes it impossible to dance to right the way through. It's peppered with lyrics that riff vaguely on the idea of time ("I can't see the time, but the time has come for sure"), and manipulation of time is key to its structure. Padding out time between the choruses are sparse, languorous verses sections that stretch out inexorably, "doubling the tempo and doubling back" as Bellotte explains it. As the track expands and contracts like a metal spring, the listener is forced into a mode of waiting, mostly for the chorus (and therefore dancing) to lurch back into action. Meanwhile, the singer bides her time, as the catty creatures of "If You Got It Flaunt It" file their talons in dark spots around the edge of the

---

[3] The title, as with many of Bellotte's songs, came out of things he commonly heard people say: people "would 'walk' or 'step' into people's lives, but this was the dance world, hence the song title." A prolific compiler of songs his whole life, he would fill "books and books full of song titles, ideas and everything," which he would go through for inspiration after he and Moroder had got a backing track together, and Moroder sung gibberish vocals over the top.

dancefloor. Hoping and waiting for her man to appear, the expansion of musical time in the verse plays against the idea of urgency. She acts as if there is all the time in the world, but when the frenzied pace of the chorus switches abruptly to panic, time closes in again. With the midnight curfew and threat of exposure creating dramatic tension, time is, of course, the ruler in many Cinderella stories. There's the slow ticking ennui of waiting for a miserable and unfulfilled life to change, and the horizonless forever of happily ever after. In Disney's 1950 version, she risks losing all by forgetting the hour and, in the lead up to midnight, falls into a trance-out-of-time, caught in the romantic circularity of the waltz. It's rather like the "party time" that one of disco's biographers, Tim Lawrence, sees disco inhabiting. "Party time" unfolds in a different dimension, suspending the normal temporal rules and, as if to underscore the idea, David Mancuso's early Loft parties were advertised with a flyer printed with Salvador Dali's melting watches. Conversely, "Dance into my Life" demonstrates a hyper-awareness of time. Fraught with anxiety, she races to snare her man by the end of the night, or else. A better-known Donna Summer song had, in fact, served as an early run through of the same scenario. Yet where "Last Dance" explored the idea with exuberant chutzpah and a feeling that everything would turn out well in the end, here there is little optimism. The clawing fear of going home alone is intense enough to bring tears to her eyes, even while she dances. In many ways, it's a more vigorous enactment of the consummate disco-angst song, The Smiths' "How Soon Is Now," where Morrissey's tortured howl takes the lonely night out to its ultimate destination—you leave on your own, you go home and you cry and you want to die.[4]

Dance isn't even allowed to be leisure here, like the marshmallow dream of Disney's 1950 Cinderella waltz "So this is Love" (originally titled "Dancing on a Cloud"); it's work, partly coded as mechanical by the sad robot vocoder that doubles the singer throughout. Vocoder was a prominent part of Moroder's armory of sound since he began experimenting with voice in the jittery, gated manipulation on the 1975 solo album *Einzelganger*. He was so attached to the technology that in the late 1970s he was given to providing demonstrations on television of how the instrument worked. As dancing machines go, this one isn't exactly the "automatic, systematic" girl admired in The Jackson 5's hit, who dances incessantly from the moment the coin drops for her own enjoyment. The stop/go routine of the character in "Dance into my Life" is enacted not out of pleasure but necessity and fear. It's a pragmatic approach to her situation, and perhaps we should be admiring her for the emotional resilience of dancing through the tears. Pete Bellotte's own reflection on the song is that it "indicates the strength in her" as she progresses through the fairy tale, but the effect is also rather . . .

---

[4]The psychodrama of failing to get into the club in the first place was explored in Paul Jabara's "Shut Out—Heaven is a Disco," which guest starred Summer in two roles: she was both fairy godmother to Jabara's hapless disco Cinderella, unable to pay his way in, and imperious gatekeeper to heaven, issuing a list of entry requirements in "Proud Mary"-era Tina Turner style. The song contains the startling couplet "open up those golden gates, here we come on roller skates," one of the gayest things disco ever produced.

well ... *desperate*. Imagine doing the bump with a new dance partner, only to find them fighting back the tears—not exactly a turn on. Apparently, though, this is the effect on Prince Charming, who unexpectedly appears obsessed with finding his bride when the curtain opens on the final Act.

And so, we arrive at the last side of the record, the final act of the play. Act 4, like Act 2, makes a virtue of the musical similarity between tracks, allowing for continuous DJ play.[5] Relentlessly upbeat until it reaches the final epilog, it houses the album's two hits, and in many ways forms the template for another "Side 4" the following year, the "MacArthur Park Suite" on the *Live And More* album. "I Love You" came first in November and performed decently in Europe, particularly the well-established territories of Germany, The Netherlands and the UK.[6] America was more hesitant to embrace singles

[5] In New York, most DJs had Acts 1, 2 and 4 on their playlists, ignoring Act 3 (although Walter Gibbons cherry picked "If You Got It Flaunt It" for his own sets). The three sides together topped Aletti's disco file top 20 for December, and featured heavily on DJ playlists through January, February, and March the following year. DJs would often list whole albums (or sides of albums) if many of the cuts were being played (and albums were mined for potential dancefloor hits as soon as they came out, regardless of whether they were being pushed as singles).

[6] If 1977 saw dwindling singles success in the US, the UK was enjoying a period of Summermania. After the huge sales of "I Feel Love," there was a rush to get as much of her material to the public as possible. Three further singles were spun off *I Remember Yesterday*, while the theme to *The Deep* was a top 5 hit. With albums just six months apart, the singles chart became cluttered with Donna Summer tracks to the point where they often competed against each other. In the autumn, label complications meant the Casablanca-issued release of "I Love You" found itself jostling in the top ten with the GTO release of "Love's Unkind" from her previous album.

from the album and only "I Love You" hit the *Billboard* Top 40, peaking at a disappointing 37. Early the following year, "Rumour Has It" followed. It did roughly similar business in Europe, but could climb no higher than 53 in America, her last single to struggle on the charts before entering a golden phase of top 5 hits ("Last Dance" in 1977 to "On The Radio" in 1979). Casablanca was certainly never a label to undersell its artists, though. In February, trying to revive interest, an elaborate three-page ad was taken out in *Billboard* for the album, announcing the single as "the most requested cut from the gold LP."

It's not too controversial to say that, musically speaking, "Rumour Has It" is one of the less interesting tracks on the album, singled out in a fair *Billboard* appraisal of the album as "not quite as creative as the other up-tempo cuts." After the variety and innovation of the previous three sides, it struggles to make its presence felt. Harmonically pretty static, throughout the introduction and verses it leans on a bass pedal (a note sustained at the bottom as different chords progress over it). These qualities worked fine in discos, though, where the pedal, low toms, and scowling clavinet wrestle the dancer to the floor. It was so effective in a yin/yang pair with the contrastingly airy "I Love You" (where bass is absent until the chorus) that many DJs at the time simply played the two songs in sequence. The transition up a fourth between the songs is a heart-lifting moment, catapulting the listener from the grounded stomp of "Rumour Has It" up into the heavens. "I Love You," as a title, echoes the minimal elegance of "I Feel Love," but presents a challenge for songwriters: How do you swerve the vortex of banality inherent in one of pop's most common song titles? "I Love You" songs have appeared in every decade and many different music markets around the world (now including K-pop) have their own takes. The big challenge is to make them less hackneyed and the swerve away from cliché has inspired some dark twists over the years. Yello's "I Love You" from 1983 severs the words from their romantic context, and by reconstituting them within a twitchy car-crash soundscape, connects them with danger. Even more disturbing is Dizzee Rascal's "I Luv U"—a vicious rap battle between a defensive pair of lovers, where robotic repetition of the title underscores how tragically dysfunctional and ill-matched the two really are. If *Once Upon A Time's* attempt isn't exactly subversive, it at least has a trick of its own to stand out from the herd; the title is repeated no less than fifty-eight times, with a further fifteen repetitions of "love you." As if by stuffing her fingers in ears and repeating the mantra to the exclusion of anything else, the singer succeeds in drowning out other outcomes of her story. "I Love You" pushes the sentiment so far that you'd be forgiven for wondering what she's really afraid of. The possibility that everlasting heterosexual love isn't what she dreamed of? Or perhaps that it doesn't really exist.

Of course, it could just be that she's happy. *Very* happy. The music joins in the monomania of the lyrics, shutting down any ambiguity. Joy freewheels from beginning to end through a harmonic and melodic organization structured like a wedding cake. Constant vertical motion sweeps the listener up sumptuously frosted tiers to the giddy crown at the summit. After a shameless two octave climb to a soaring string instrumental section, you can almost visualize the aerial camera shot revolving around the happy couple planted in the top tier fondant. From here on out of the song, the final thirty seconds glide weightlessly on a held string chord, with clavinet fluttering around like clouds of birds. It's a magnificent moment, and a delicate final flourish to a number that overall is brutally effective rather than subtle. There's still something missing around what should be a climactic point in the story, though. In many Cinderella stories, this is the moment of highest dramatic tension for Cinderella—will she or won't she be found by the prince? Can she overcome the final hurdle to fulfil her destiny? *Once Upon A Time's* heroine faces no major obstacle to her love, no imprisonment or trial of authenticity. The buoyant mood of "Rumour Has It" flattens out any tension within the trial, making the happy ending an all but foregone conclusion. If you were paying attention to the lyrics of the song—and the diction of Summer's strained soprano scarcely helps the words come across—you'd discover that getting the man ultimately isn't a just reward for her hard work and trials. It's simply inescapable destiny. In dramatic terms, this is a diminishment, and belittles much of the angst wrung out of the previous three acts. It's probably a blessing that the musical was never produced—despite its masterful musical sequencing, the album doesn't really work as conventional drama. Having said that, what Act 4 manages, in its romp home over the finishing line of love, is to capture the atmosphere of the closing numbers of a rock show or juke box musical: the audience get the stuff they want (or at least what the producers think they want) and are sent home happy with feel-good tunes ringing in their ears. What comes next after the twin-pack of singles continues this feeling, but by this point the music has completely given up on drama, content just to serve up a jubilant mood. "Happy Ever After" is effectively the curtain call, a feel-good finale hollowed out of lyrical content so that the cast can be dragged back on stage to receive their applause.

It's the disco version of what happens at the end of a more conventional fairy-tale musical: the happy couple, finally united, are cheered triumphantly into the sunset, while the credits start to roll. The musical tradition established in the 1950s (the Disney *Cinderella's,* as well as the Rodgers and Hammerstein musical) was to send the couple off with heavenly choirs, swelling strings, and fanfares.[7] In *Once Upon A Time*, we get an appropriate update for the 1970s—a shimmering façade of sound that drips with the opulence of a chi-chi shopping mall. Frothy cascades of Rhodes piano foam like champagne waterfalls over imported marble, the aural equivalent of the opening titles of the TV series *Dynasty*. What the track is lacking in depth and story, it makes up by assaulting the listener with sheer gloss. This kind of *disco-luxe,* verging on easy listening, is almost a sub-genre of disco in itself (think of the Barry White-produced "Love's Theme" or Johnny Mathis pouring his velvet and cream vocals over orchestral disco covers of Cole Porter).

With so much aural confetti thrown in the listeners' ears, it's easy to become distracted from a central issue in the story. After fifteen songs we know an awful lot about the singer and

---

[7] It actually wasn't until the 1990s that Disney's animated movies introduced the sounds that signify the passage into deathly domesticity—church bells.

her desires, but what do we know about the *object* of her desire? Who is the "he" to whom "Happily Ever After" constantly makes reference? What have we learned about him in over an hour of music-time? The answer, of course, is absolutely nothing. Prince Charming is just a bit part in the joy Cinderella has confected around herself, given no characteristics of his own. She may as well be singing to a pumpkin. If I'm tempted to speculate that he doesn't exist, that's because he's at best an abstraction who fails to leave a footprint on the story. But then isn't this true to some extent of almost all Cinderella stories? We're so conditioned now (with Disney partly to blame) to think of Cinderella as a romantic fantasy, that we've hit a blind spot: the biggest hook for the audience isn't romance, but the heroine ascending out of her dire situation to a new one that befits her worth. We don't cheer her for finding the man of her dreams, we're mostly relieved that she doesn't have to sleep in a fireplace any more. Now, we can rest easy knowing that her exterior circumstances match what we know to be her interior qualities—kind, good, deserving of social status. All the while, we can also enjoy the schadenfreude (where kind and generous Cinderella cannot) of witnessing the comeuppance of her tormentors. Still, there is the nagging doubt—if she can't tell us anything about the man, are her feelings pure projection?

Finally, just as with Charles Perrault's story, the listener isn't allowed to depart without one last moral being delivered, in case we hadn't grasped the real meaning of the story. "Happily Ever After," it turns out, isn't the real ending, but a false one. The final, final curtain is a reprise of the opening title track, in line with the closing tracks of most of Summer's previous albums. On some of these albums, the use of reprises can have a tendency to feel perfunctory, tacked on the end to bring the sense of a grander scheme without the real structural work having been done. But this isn't at all true for the two reprises of "Once Upon A Time," which draw the listener back into the essential tragedy of the story and prevent it from getting too carefree. The final mournful piano revision of the theme is the backdrop for a monolog, which is startlingly overwrought to the point of high camp. The message—if you believe hard enough your dreams will come true—is straightforward enough, although, as with "I Love You," the central idea "so she dreamed" is hammered home through brute repetition, almost to the point of hysteria. The message is also fundamentally identical to the opening song of the Disney animation, "A Dream Is A Wish Your Heart Makes," where your dreams can come true "no matter how your heart is grieving, if you keep on believing." Disney's Cinderella manages to stay chipper, despite the grief of losing her father and being effectively forced into slavery. In contrast, "(Theme) Once Upon A Time" reverses the polarity of the message from winsome to heart-wrenching. As an epilog, after the prize has been won, the low circumstances left behind, why is the ending so desperately sad? Finally comes Summer's forlorn soprano, repeating the melody of the theme one last time—a desolate sob into the void. If the goal has been (seemingly) achieved, what is this trying to tell us? That the scars of tragedy never completely heal? That there are a million other lonely suffering Cinderella's out there? At least it rescues the story from a trite ending—the girl dancing off into the golden evening with her anonymous paramour—that doesn't feel earned.

You may disagree with my interpretations of events, and that's fine—understandable really. It's almost certainly not what its writers and singer intended. At the end of the story, though, what you or I make of it is up to us. Many times I have rippled the waters of *Once Upon A Time* just to find out what comes back. When the image settles, what I usually see is myself staring back. It's beautiful and sad and, yes, probably very self-indulgent. What is it that you see?

# Happily Ever After—An Invitation

If there's one single reason why this book came about it's this—*Once Upon A Time* is a masterclass in storytelling through pop music. In many ways, you can open it up and listen as if you were turning the pages of a children's storybook—clean, simple, uncomplicated. In other ways, it is endlessly layered, giving you reasons to read it again and again. But it is imperfect. Like the best and most rewarding texts, it doesn't always make sense. And unlike the movies, which at least fool you into believing you are watching seamless, real life, it gives you an incomplete picture. The pieces of information that are missing keep many of its meanings elusive, the interpretations multiple. Part of what makes the best stories so compelling is how you insert yourself into them. You can, as I and others have done, fill the gaps with your own experience as you go along through life. For me, a lot of this happened as I discovered my sexual identity, and the difficulties of fitting into the night world that *Once Upon A Time* portrays. For another person, it will be a very different story. Then again, you might just love the album because it makes you want to dance. It's really good at that too.

However you feel about *Once Upon A Time*, imagine. Make it your own.

# Also available in the series

18. *The Rolling Stones' Exile on Main St.* by Bill Janovitz

19. *The Beach Boys' Pet Sounds* by Jim Fusilli

20. *Ramones' Ramones* by Nicholas Rombes

21. *Elvis Costello's Armed Forces* by Franklin Bruno

22. *R.E.M.'s Murmur* by J. Niimi

23. *Jeff Buckley's Grace* by Daphne Brooks

24. *DJ Shadow's Endtroducing. . . . .* by Eliot Wilder

25. *MC5's Kick Out the Jams* by Don McLeese

26. *David Bowie's Low* by Hugo Wilcken

27. *Bruce Springsteen's Born in the U.S.A.* by Geoffrey Himes

28. *The Band's Music from Big Pink* by John Niven

29. *Neutral Milk Hotel's In the Aeroplane over the Sea* by Kim Cooper

30. *Beastie Boys' Paul's Boutique* by Dan Le Roy

31. *Pixies' Doolittle* by Ben Sisario

32. *Sly and the Family Stone's There's a Riot Goin' On* by Miles Marshall Lewis

33. *The Stone Roses' The Stone Roses* by Alex Green

34. *Nirvana's In Utero* by Gillian G. Gaar

35. *Bob Dylan's Highway 61 Revisited* by Mark Polizzotti

36. *My Bloody Valentine's Loveless* by Mike McGonigal

37. *The Who's The Who Sell Out* by John Dougan

38. *Guided by Voices' Bee Thousand* by Marc Woodworth

39. *Sonic Youth's Daydream Nation* by Matthew Stearns

40. *Joni Mitchell's Court and Spark* by Sean Nelson

41. *Guns N' Roses' Use Your Illusion I and II* by Eric Weisbard

42. *Stevie Wonder's Songs in the Key of Life* by Zeth Lundy

# Index